(un)common:
anthology of new Welsh writing

LUCENT DREAMING

First Edition

(un)common: anthology of new Welsh writing
Published by Lucent Dreaming Ltd.
103 Bute Street, Cardiff, CF10 5AD

ISBN 978-1-9166320-5-9

Lucent Dreaming acknowledges the support of Literature Wales
and the financial support of Books Council of Wales and Creative Wales.

Llenyddiaeth
Cymru
Literature
Wales

CYNGOR LLYFRAU CYMRU
BOOKS COUNCIL of WALES

All the anthology's contributors were a part of Literature Wales' 2022–23 Representing Wales programme.

Literature Wales is the national company for the development of literature whose vision is a Wales where literature empowers, improves and brightens lives.

Contents

(un)common

Introduction

Rosy Adams & Alix Edwards

Common: general, not specific; familiar, not pretentious
Common also: ordinary, not excellent, not distinguished,
belonging to the masses
In common: shared

What we have in common as writers, no matter what life
has thrown us, or where we are today, is that we all grew to
adolescence in underprivileged households.

Chosen to participate in the Representing Wales/
Cynrychioli Cymru 2022/23 writer development
programme for underrepresented writers, run by
Literature Wales/Llenyddiaeth Cymru, we tread the
common ground of "not having". But our lives are very
different and each of our voices spins a different tale.

Kittie Belltree's sequence of poems, "elegy for
estranged sisters after inclement weather", after the image

"Cloud Sisters" by Maggie Taylor, tells a story of estranged sisters. Her words are carefully patterned and stitched, underscoring the needlecraft imagery in the text. The stormy weather and turbulent family relationships strain against the containment of societal and poetic structure, creating an unbearable tension.

In "The Hand that Makes the Sound", "Lamb" and "Slipstream" Anthony Shapland's protagonists are set apart from others. They struggle to fit in a world that seems alien to them. Through disguise and imitation they survive, without expectation of anything more, but there is a chance of recognition and connection where they least expect it.

The poems of Frankie Parris have a dreamlike quality, an edge of reality feeling, as if only the things that you look at directly are solid and unmoving. Out the corners of your eyes things are mutable, and the moment you look away everything changes. Past, present and future collide. Their world is familiar yet uncertain. They clutch at sensory moments and everyday routines but still do not belong.

"The Man in the Living Room" by Jon Doyle is a chilling story of the consequences of unquestioning belief in an age of information overload, and the circumstances which can make any one of us vulnerable.

Ciaran Keys' "Nervosa" explores stuckness, depression, anxiety and addiction, all linked like a Möbius strip, as consequences of feeling like a human by-product of the stagnant world in which he finds himself growing up. He captures the surreal qualities of dissociation and ennui that dominate our conscious mind when we can't see a way forward, and the challenges to be overcome on the journey to regain our sense of self.

Amy Kitcher's first story, "Darkness Brighter than the Sun", features the transformation of veteran soldiers from two generations, bringing to mind the legendary cauldron of rebirth within which dead warriors could be restored to life. The second, "New Year's Eve at The Nun's Purse", is set in what may well be the worst pub in the whole of the British Isles on New Year's Eve, when love, birth, pain and death all make their mark before the sun rises.

In "Danny in the Dragon's Den", an extract from her children's novel of the same title, Simone Greenwood tackles grief, hunger, and the upside-down world of the young carer who has to look after the person who is meant to look after them, as well as questioning the role of the narrator in children's novels. Danny is resilient and funny and kind, and he finds an unusual friend to talk to in these five chapters. Simone's series of poems "Into the Blackwood: character sketches from the Valleys" are conversational, a dialogue in which she carefully frames her characters so they become like a collection of portraits.

Bridget Keehan's racing narrative, "The Changing Room", is an extract from her novel *Identity Theft*. It stands alone as a complete short story, within which the young protagonist moulds herself to meet the expectations of her father, unconventional though they may be.

Alix Edwards' "Fifty Miles an Hour" also explores the relationship between a daughter and her father: how one moment can change everything, as the loss of a parent's income can plunge a whole family into poverty. Her poems trace the progression of romantic love from heady honeymoon days to moments of violence, loneliness and regret.

Ben Huxley's "Winter Wynn Gardens" is like a documentary; a day in the life of the titular Gardens, in which we follow the paths, observing characters as they come and go, without attachment or judgement.

"Blodeuwedd on the 28" by Anastacia Ackers gives a voice to the woman made of flowers in a delightful story that weaves Welsh myth into the ordinary routine of present day life in the style of a traditional storyteller. Her "Manifesto" closes this anthology with a creative call to arms.

Rosy Adams also contributes two contemporary stories that draw heavily on myth and fairy tales: "Tower Block Rapunzel" seeks to humanise the characters of this tale and explores the consequences of their choices. No-one is wholly good or bad, right or wrong. "The Green Coat" is about transformation, the inevitable eruption of the true self when cultural conditioning and pharmaceutical restraints can no longer contain it.

Read on, and you will discover (un)common worlds. There are dragons, cloud-circling and deep-dwelling. Characters travel by bus and by train. They walk, run or even fly, through the pin-drop silence of libraries, through moon-frosted streets and winter-chilled parks, farms, houses, shops, cafés, and possibly the grottiest pub in existence.

Family ties are important, and not always the ones you're born with. Transformation can liberate but also imprison us. We encounter isolation, addiction, tragedy and grief, but we also find love, connection, and hope.

Rosy Adams and Alix Edwards
Llangeitho and Cardiff, July 2023

(un)common

elegy for estranged sisters after inclement weather

After the image "Cloud Sisters" by Maggie Taylor

Kittie Belltree

i.

the storm is over everything like a knife in the galley kitchen
tempest strips cupboards bare stomachs are removed as part
of a thumbs down on picnics and holidays we have no food
to share and must stare at each other from opposite ends of

an empty table the storm says form an orderly line where the
roof leaks in our bedroom it's raining walking sticks and crosses
funny how we speak of the weather like a friend how there are
no words only atmospheric conditions as mother cuts the frenum
with a gust of disapproval: *this is how I lost you*

ii.

my childhood a needle in a mud storm
i ache to understand why
> *for a few pins and a new dress*
you stood steadfast as the needle she stuck in my throat

i ache to understand why
the night mother stripped you from me like a muddy dress
> *you stood steadfast as the needle she stuck in my throat*
it was raining pinpricks and crosses inside the empty wardrobe

the night mother stripped you from me like a muddy dress
i remember you mouthing something
> *it was raining pinpricks and crosses inside the empty wardrobe*
how your thin voice drowned in the downpour of silence
inbred

i remember you mouthing something
and the needle-sharp shriek of grief flooding veins
> *how your thin voice drowned in the downpour of silence inbred*
i can still taste the ribbons of blood you pinned on my tongue

and the needle-sharp shriek of grief flooding veins
for a few pins and a new dress
> *i can still taste the ribbons of blood you pinned on my tongue*
my childhood a needle in a mud storm

iii.

how is the weather where you are? / *before the mud storm and the needle split*
I'm only thinking of you today because / *I had a sister*
I'm wearing that vintage dress / *sewn inside my heart*
I pinched from your wardrobe / *where it never rains but pours*
I'm thinner than you so / *I miss you so bad*
It looks better on me anyway / *I ache like a floodplain*
trust me, I'm a doctor now / *but that's just me being selfish*
this means I know everything / *is what mother said*
and have no interest in your opinions / *before she unpicked the stitches*

The Hand that Makes the Sound

Anthony Shapland

Lying low in the unmown garden, she makes herself invisible, the way she can.

The quiet man is here again. He touches the peak of his cap in greeting, she's still seen – motionless, she shuts eyes tight, and grips the long, wiry grass. Sunlight blinks red in her dark, leaves rustle above her head. She hears him knock at the door, as he does every morning, three knocks that never raise an answer.

She peeks. He nods with a smile. Maybe they are invisible together, she thinks.

She doesn't remember when he first came, or a day he hasn't. Her curiosity leans toward him, standing tall, like a tree. He lifts the letterbox to post a creased envelope.

From her place in the grass an unnamed game is forgotten. Hands stopped mid-air, holding toys and dirt-filled plastic cups. Eyes follow him as he makes his way along the road. He carries a bag. It's a funny shape, like a fat sausage. A cloth with dabs of colour is tied around the curved handle like a flag. Things stick out of the sausage-bag, plenty in it to play with – long wooden rulers, brushes and a drumstick. At least, it looks like a drumstick for a big drum, or a gong.

He turns the corner. She feels left behind, puzzled and cross.

He never carries a gong.

Or a drum.

—

A man stands with arms outstretched, his head bows, hands droop, feet splay. Dyna'r silwét yma. Dim ond aros – just waiting, standing at the beginning, my scarecrow. Yn dawel. Patient. Staring at the ground, mae wedi colli rhywbeth —

He loads the brush with paint. Long fibres bend in a tight curve where they meet the surface. A light ground and a black, fluid line.

What is it you've lost?

He is the signwriter. Signs that say what people want them

to say, set tangible and real in the flow of his brush. A copyist, he sees structure, pattern, a curve fully-formed in the air. He traces it, makes its edge definite.

His hand gives voice to the town.

His hand tells you the miles to the next village, says if the toilet is vacant or occupied, or which cuts of meat are on *special*. He puts names *&Co* above shops. His are the notices that tell you where to go, which Biblical quote to heed in fear, or ignore at peril. In an exchange of money and language *Sunnymede* overpaints *Gwynfa*.

Each day, he appears –
along the terrace to her house, quiet and constant
through the lazy dog-days of sun, envelopes and smiles
                    – then disappears.

The long weeks of summer leave her alone, the house is quiet, empty of children. Just her, left behind. She drifts a little in idleness, drifts a little toward play, and waits for the quiet man to return.

He appears in her made-up world. A fairground game; toys and plastic clothes-pegs, twigs and buckets' animated swoop and crash. Jaunty music keeps time in the breeze of her imagined soundtrack. The tall, quiet man is the boss. He operates the rides and has jewels and magic that make social workers explode, grown-ups melt. Spins them so hard their heads fly off.

One morning, slowly then all at once, she's bored of being on her own.

A gloss-black beetle moves awkwardly under toys, over grass, and the excitement of the game fades into a lawn of bright plastic litter. It feels childish. Clouds threaten morning rain but she resists going inside.

The air is heavy.

Perhaps he isn't coming back. Perhaps she imagined him after all. She climbs the tree on the corner and waits for him to pass below, to make sure he's real – to peer into the sausage-bag at curled silver tubes and shiny tins and even more interesting sticks.

–

A hoop. A large gold hoop in soft earlobes. A large round gold hoop that shines with the same fine light that glows in the hairs of the soft earlobes that belong to the landlady of The Ship – Gloria. Glorious Gloria. Y geindeg Gloria yn gloywi, gloyw fel glo gleision.

That's the next sound, held by its edges, formed at its middle.

Curry night at *The Ship*. Pub Quiz rollover. Gloria reads out this week's menu. What's to eat, the price of drinks, karaoke. Karaoke. She says the last word again – her fingers bounce along it on the page, he watches her lips. *Caru-o-ci.*

She hands over the list, as agreed – and writes down exactly what she wants. He looks at the shapes, examines then underlines it in pen as received and understood. They do one last check that the order is right, the spelling is right. Because, *the customer is always right*.

She knows. Knows that he doesn't hear what she hears in written words. Mostly he has learnt how to be, to operate without anyone noticing. Guesses hit their mark. He nods. Open, sincere, agreeable. Cautious.

On the wooden stepladder he settles with brushes and paint, his familiar place at the noticeboard. A crow's nest.

The pub fills below. He returns greetings, but never initiates conversation. He smooths over his evasiveness, concentrates on tapping out guidelines in chalk. People don't pry. He knows when to work and he knows when to be silent. Always polite. He waits for them to stop asking questions, a tide that will pass.

Soul, bowl, shoal, whole.

Ie, dyma siâp hwn. Hoop shape, round as the sun and shining, a round pint glass beer-run-froth, round tables, round bar stools and dartboards –

– Bullseye.

–

She didn't do it, she says.

She did.

Stealing food. Silently – proudly – prising open the noisy biscuit-barrel. Shut in her room, grounded until she owns up. Pockets grit in guilt sweet crumb. One day she'll run away, then auntie will be sorry for being mean. She decides what to take, packing and re-packing. Not my auntie anyway, *any* child's auntie. She can't remember when she realised that auntie isn't a relative or that *The Home* isn't the same as *home*. The other children disappear one by one, all their belongings removed. Now it's just her.

In small revenge she moves stuff around *The Home*, returns books to shelves upside-down, un-sets clocks, pushes pictures from true.

She takes a key for the front door. Hides it in a sock,
      in a glove,
in a toy.

Between mealtimes, unmissed and unrepentant, she makes her escape. She wonders where the quiet man's home is, trails behind him, shy, at a distance. Bolder, she dares herself further and further. Learns his route.

He walks past the houses each morning. She tracks the scent of tobacco and work-clothes across a park, pulls herself tall to roll with the same gait. She steps where he steps, looks where he looks, stops when he stops. If he turns, she's a sightless stone lion. She still wonders if only she can see him, or he her. He slows, she slows, along a row of workshops. He bends low, a roller shutter opens in a metallic screech and rumble. He ducks inside.

She expects him to emerge. But he doesn't. She plays nearby, in the rust and dust of the lane between makeshift garages. Waiting.

–

Climbing up one side to tumble down the mountain. Two mounds with a deep trough between the slopes, the river ribbons cut a rock-meander outside the old house. Gartref yn fy nyffryn i. Wiggling toes inside socks, cofio'r cawodydd glaw, i lawr a bant â fi. Dyma fi lan, lawr, lan a lawr.

She watches from the lane. Her hands shade bright sunlight and the interior is cooler, darker. At the centre, a large busy table, a pool of amber light where his attention rests. He's surrounded by pots and jars of paint on shelves. Pegboards prop bright paintings to dry. Letter-curls, richly painted words and gold dropshadows, a fairground sheen, a rhythm amongst the brushes and pens and pencils, beneath a pinboard shivering with scraps and flaps of paper, like bunting.

— my up, down, up, and down.

Softer, softly after rain, a smaller climb. Two molehills. Over the valley at home, to warm my face, round as the sun that rises —

She keeps her distance across the lane. Garage workers

come and go all day. Cars rise up on hydraulic lifts, the radio jabbers. They tell her to go home. Where are her parents? A polystyrene cup of sugary tea. She doesn't speak, a well-practised, innocent, infuriating silence. One by one they tire of babysitting.

She stares at the signwriter. He's somehow softer at work, crumpled, like her favourite sweatshirt, chewed and familiar. Auntie said to stop bothering him, stop bothering *HalfTom*. She stares – in that way she's been told not to at strangers. He isn't a stranger, the quiet man. He has a tooth missing at one side and green paint in his hair that was there yesterday.

She breathes in the workshop smell, pungent like medicine, oily as plasticine or kitchen lino. Waxy, like shoes warmed by feet. She likes it.

In the late afternoon, moths spiral and dive around the glowing bulb but his eye is fixed at the tip of the brush.

–

Mae'r haul yn codi, but the second circle is the moon. The other earlobe, the hoop and Gloria's laugh. Two. Dwy. Dwy linell grom sy'n cwrdd yn gywir. Two curves complete the round.

She watches and listens, smiling.

Those three symbols together turn my valley into an owl. A beak and eyes. Blank and searching, unblinking. Pig a llygaid. Beth wyt ti wedi'i golli, dylluan fach?

His routine is her routine that summer. At her door each morning, as the envelope hits the mat, he nods then she nods. Day by day, little by little, the distance closes. Soon she walks at his side. Today she walks into the workshop. The arrangement settles around them both, subtle as a gentle breeze on a calm day, or a warm current in a cool stream.

—

Please, he insists, it is much better if you write it down. Letter by letter.

The customer sighs and pulls paper toward him. She watches. It's a game, she understands, like a spell. Everything must be memorised, repeated. Agreed.

Only then he begins. When he is at his table alone he sees it, the whole. The rise and the fall of curves, sharp angles and hard lines, he knows how it should sit on the sign, how it should hold a rhythm in space, a pause, before the industry of brushes and movement. The words are made solid, repeatable from rounded lips. Her mouth shapes vowels and turns around consonants, the sound of each letter sings in her mind.

But not in *his*.

Something is stuck. He hears and understands well

enough. The flow of his first tongue breaks on the banks of pebbles, which clack and bowl together in the adopted round nouns of the town.

Sounds begin and end in speech, unrelated to the shapes he copies every day. He looks at the marks on a page and they make no music. The marriage is troubled. It doesn't add up to anything. It never has. Even now they sit as squiggles and glyphs, but remain disconnected. Silent.

As they walk he lists all the signs he must paint today, who they are for, and where they will end up.

Unasked she reads his next-day jobs from scraps of paper. She repeats them aloud, navigating new, slow words. *Two-can-dine-for-nine-ninety-nine* and he wonders if she knows what they mean, the letters that make the words, so she explains them to him in new pictures. He listens carefully. He doesn't use a funny voice when he speaks to her. Not like the other grown-ups.

She wonders what the opposite of disappearing feels like.

Usually, her grown-ups never really explain what they mean. They talk in that. Slow. Loud. Way. they use to explain things. They talk behind hands about the brown envelopes, about *keep* from the brother. She is puzzled. It doesn't make sense. In the home-not-home where auntie isn't her auntie – whose brother?

A thought arrives. Her voice flutters in her throat, she

skips a little with the new idea then sudden fury bursts. *Mine?* Grown-ups flush red, fold towels briskly and don't look at her. She feels clever, like she has found her way back to a place she has been before. She has known him all her life, but he only met her when he was already grown.

She doesn't have a mother tongue. Or a father tongue, but she has a brother tongue. Or, as the grown-ups call him now, a *half*-brother tongue.

—

My hand must move like a snake. Not the adders on the hill that coil, and not the grass snakes' quick smooth lines beneath slate.

Pa ffordd mae'n symud nawr? Its tail starts here at my brush hand and curves away from my grip before coming down and back again, yn ôl ac ymlaen. Yna mae'n troi i edrych bant, tuag at fy llaw arall.

It must — this slippery thing — it must look back toward the hoop. The snake looks up at the moon. Mae'r lleuad yn syllu ar y neidr.

A pause. The stub of a pencil fits a tooth-left gap in the corner of his mouth. He swaps it for a cigarette, sparks, squints at progress.

She sits and watches the ritual. Her copycat pencil-end draws moisture from her mouth, gnawed into wet splinters and cool sweet graphite. From the soft chair in the doorway, she watches her brother. This soft chair that is now *her* chair.

White smoke curls.

The thinned paint slides like cream from a spoon.

In a row they stand, my scarecrow, the hoop, my valley and O, a setting sun watched by the snake. TOMOS. It's my sign. Fy enw i, fy arwydd i. A signwriter's sign.

The long hairs soft and flexible, a satisfying resistance under pressure. His wrist sits on the mahlstick and, from the tip of his fingers, he thinks through the glide of the liquid from the reservoir between fibres. Every day she brings new words into his silence. She speaks the signs he makes, and sounds flow with his brush. He controls the turn, the sweep and the stop; all at a speed that allows the pigment to settle, the line to smooth and her voice to resonate.

Tower Block Rapunzel

Rosy Adams

This is how it begins. She sits on the balcony, among the washing lines and plant pots. She is brushing her hair. It soothes her. The long, firm sweep of the brush. The tug on her scalp as it drags out the tangles. Her hair is glossy and reddish, like the skin of a conker. When she stands it reaches the backs of her knees.

When it rains she watches TV. Mama brings her books from the library and magazines from the corner shop. She doesn't really like to read but it makes Mama happy when she tries. Mostly she sits on the balcony and talks to the birds.

Seagulls and starlings, pigeons and sparrows, jackdaws and crows. She feeds them and talks to them, and they talk to her in turn. The crows bring her gifts: pennies, pebbles, pieces of glass, a single silver earring. She keeps them all in a jewellery box in her bedroom.

When she is bored (which is often) she makes patterns. She makes them everywhere; out of rice grains, lentils, and pasta shapes, or little stones and shells that Mama brings her from the seashore. On her own skin, with soft tipped pens, a riot of colours all over her arms and legs. Fresh ink over faded, day after week after month after year, and underneath are other patterns, all fine silver-white lines. She keeps those hidden. She's not supposed to have sharp things, but she was given a fountain pen for her twelfth birthday so she could write a daily diary. Something about being good for her mental health. She spent long hours filing the nib into a minuscule blade. It's no good for using on paper anymore.

Rachael: in films it's always like, the real mother is perfect, but she dies when the princess is a baby, and then she ends up with a wicked stepmother who treats her like trash. My life must be back to front because my real mother was a smack head who didn't care enough about me to stop using while she was pregnant. My dad was just as bad. They were broke as shit and desperate, so the old man, he decided it would be a good idea to nick some of his neighbour's supply, who was dealing in kilos. He thought they wouldn't miss a little bit. Dumb junkie logic. He told himself a little story about how it would all be ok, but it wasn't.

They caught him. Of course they did. They couldn't let him get away with it, so they gave him a beating, but they beat him a bit too hard. He died of internal bleeding, on his own bedroom floor, with my mother in the bed, so off her face that she didn't even notice. Lucky for her she was so obviously pregnant with me, or they might have given her the same treatment.

By the time she came down enough to realise what had happened they were long gone, and every trace of them had been scrubbed from the house next door. I think she lost it then. There was certainly no way she could look after me. They packed her off to the loony bin, and that's where I was born, a little junkie baby. As far as I know she's still there.

Once I'd gone through withdrawal they put me up for adoption, and that's how Mama ended up with me. Sometimes I wonder if she regrets taking me on. Knowing what she knows now, would she do it again? I'm afraid to ask.

Mama: It's not always been easy. But not for one moment have I regretted taking on the little scrap. And little she was. Pale and undersized, already with a mop of fine, flyaway hair like a dandelion clock. It went dark and silky as she got older, but for her first year it stayed ash blonde.

She could be lovely sometimes, but I never knew what she was going to do when the mood was on her. If a thought came into her head she would say it. If she wanted to do something she'd do it. That's why I kept her away from other people. I thought I was doing the right thing. Now I'm not so sure.

Every weekday Mama goes out to work. Every morning when she leaves the flat, she locks the door behind her. There is a maintenance man who doubles as a supervisor for the whole building. If there happens to be an emergency he can unlock the door when Mama is at work. He can unlock any of the doors. But each day is more or less the same.

Let's take a closer look at the maintenance man. He has a small room on the ground floor where he can go on his breaks and drink tea in front of a little gas fire. He's probably in his thirties but he looks older. He wears a short beard, dark, but speckled with silver like his hair. He's the type of man that runs to fat in later years, but so far the physicality of his job keeps him trim, although his shoulders are bulky with muscle.

He has a small portable television in his room, but recently its screen has stayed dark. He prefers to smoke a roll-up by the open window. Across the central courtyard, about four floors up, there is a balcony. Of course there is, because all the flats above the ground floor have balconies, but this one is the only one he has eyes for. Every day a young woman sits out there, for hours at a time, talking to the birds who balance on the balcony rail and take treats from her hand.

Lately, he has begun to feel haunted. She is in his head, even when he sleeps. He neglects his work and stands by his window so he can gaze up at her.

One day, when the sight of her is no longer enough, he sneaks up to the flat when her mother has left for work. He sits with his ear pressed against the wood of the door, listening to the little rustlings and tappings from the other side, picturing her moving about, picking things up, putting them down again. He taps. Knock-knock. Knock-knock. As he waits, his heart knock-knocks against the inside of his chest. Inside, the rustlings stop and there is a listening silence.

She knocks back.

Rachael: He was the first man I ever met for real. I knew about men, or I thought I did. I might've been stuck in the flat all the time but I still had TV. No internet though, Mama didn't trust me with that.

He wasn't like I thought he'd be though. The smell of him. It took me by surprise. I was on edge, to start. It was so different. But it was... I don't know how to describe it. I wanted to bury my nose in the soft skin of his throat and take great big breaths of him. But that was later.

To begin with, there was only the voice on the other side of the door. A deep voice, with a bit of a growl underneath it. It sounded like corduroy, bitter chocolate, and tobacco. For hours, for days, all we did was talk, while Mama was out at work.

Arthur: I knew it was wrong. I could lie and say I only wanted to talk to her. Maybe I wanted to find out why she never came out of the flat. But it was much more than that. I tried to resist, but it was like she'd hypnotised me. And at the end, I just couldn't let her go. I wanted her to understand, I had to be near her for always. And even though I can never see her again, she still owns my heart. She always will.

Rachael: we had a routine. Every day, as soon as Mama had gone out, he would tap at my door. We would sit on the floor, me inside and him in the hallway, and we'd talk for hours. Then one day he told me he could unlock the door. I didn't even stop to think about what might go wrong. I didn't want to think about that. I told myself it was ok, I wasn't going out. I was just going to let him in.

Would I have done the same if it had been someone else? Probably. Can you blame me? I'd been shut in for so long. I wanted the feel of someone's skin on mine, the taste of it on my tongue. I didn't think of him as a person, with feelings. I wasn't ready for that. It was fine at first, but he wanted so much of me. More than I wanted to give.

I panicked.

I know what I did was wrong. I know that now, but I wasn't thinking straight then. I wasn't thinking at all. I just wanted him to go away and leave me alone, like Mama does when I throw a fit. But he wouldn't.

So here we are. Everyone loses.

Mama: I should have realised what was going on. I could tell something was different. I suppose I was hoping it was her age. Age does make a difference, with some things. When I came home after work she was calm. Two weeks with no outbursts at all. I should have paid closer attention. I should have questioned her, but I wanted to believe she was getting better.

That day. I'll never forget it, for the rest of my life. I walked into the flat. I was already worried because the door was unlocked. The door which I locked every morning when I left for work. And then I saw what was inside. I can still see it every time I close my eyes. But at least I still have eyes. Not like poor Arthur.

Rachael: It's not so bad here. I'm used to being locked in anyway. They can't medicate me because it might harm the babies, so they keep me away from the other patients in case I hurt someone. It's funny though, I've felt really chilled recently. I haven't had a fit since the big one. I wonder if it's the hormonal changes? It's like, whatever glitch there is in my brain has gone. Too late now, though. They're never going to let me out of this place after what I did.

Mama visits me every week. She tells me she's been feeding my birds, and she brings me the twists of silver foil and shiny stones the crows leave. She takes away the only thing I can give them now; the hacked off braid of my hair for lining their nests.

(un)common

Lamb

Anthony Shapland

He is used to Tad's work. Polythene sheeting hangs in this bay. He watches sometimes. This bit of the farm is quiet, it smells like metal and salt, less like cud or shit.

They call him the quiet one. His brothers tease him. Thirteen next month and the youngest of six. He arrived after a pause and they five were already a tribe. He senses he is different from his brothers. He tries to copy how they are, he does what they do, to slip by, unnoticed, fitting in.

Mammy's boy, laugh the lads together.

She looks out for him, keeps him close. Breathes him deep. Her youngest, her surprise, her own. The baby.

Seasons move slow, steady as they pass. They are what they are. The wait for a better year next year – or for the rain, or for the hay, the calves, the feed – the clock slowly moves forward. Time is long and unforgiving.

Some things must happen fast.

The lamb is limp over Tad's hand. Draped as he moves across the yard. He lays it on the bench and sets to. A slice along the belly that still has a cord on it and a red bloom. Up around the neck and all around a tiny head wet with slick and fluid. The tongue lolls, too big. The metal point traces the collars of its legs. Blade flat he raises the stillborn to pull back. A clean sound of layers separating. The carcass, red and small steams from the fleece.

A starling pours out it's borrowed stuttering song.

A dark clot pinks the rain-wet.

The skin is limp over Tad's hand. An empty costume. Deftly he rights a wobbling lamb, slips this loose skin onto it and ties it under the belly with twine, rubs the small body all over with hay and the chemical codes of the new skin coat.

The ewe has lost blood. He offers the new clothed lamb. She finds it, finds a scent her instinct recognises, and starts to clean it as her own.

"Lamb" is an extract from Meantime, part of Inclusive Journalism's anthology Cymru & I *(Seren, 2023)*

Poems

Frankie Parris

Sympathy for the Abyss

A year later and the phrase still swirls in my head like two-day old coffee
poured down the drain.
I saw a spider crawl out, past the edge of the cup and take refuge
under the rim.
I should have seen it as a possibility for change,
a life saved.
But no, I got jealous and left the room.
I suppose it wasn't quite as bad as flushing the poor guy down the
plug hole
but still.
Occasionally, I feel hope in my body.
I wouldn't describe it as calm, but it's as close as I can really get.
The most recent batch was feeling autumn in the air.
Nights creeping closer,
life flooding back into my fingers and wrists.
I spent a day washing and folding all my jumpers so they'd be
ready for the first frost.
Now I'm sleeping until 4pm and dreading the light appearing again.
I'd like to sharpen my edges,
lose the empathy and lose the need to throw it all away.
I'm told you can learn something from every experience, but I don't.
I let things slip down the street and into the road, ready for the
next set of wheels.
I want to be loved and
I want to be alone
and as I'm sure you can tell,
these things will never get along.

My dog won't even look at me

You bumble along, wondering who or what is going to
    take you out,
But no-one looks you in the face and tells you,
"It's you! It's you and your stupid need for validation!"
So I imagine New York,
Or San Francisco,
And sunglasses are always present,
But you aren't.
And I don't know how to get there,
Especially alone,
And every time I try,
My feet are buried even deeper in the ground.

I sip from your glass when you're out of the room,
Did you know that?

Cotswold House

I'm sitting in a room with a huge table.
There are only two of us in the room.
We don't need a huge table.
When she tells me I need to go to the hospital,
the table gets bigger.
Wider and wider it stretches.
It's sharpest edge pushes into my stomach and traps me
    against the wall.
There is a whole ocean of air between us
yet I still can't breathe properly.
She says Tuesday.
It's currently Friday.
I have four days to plan my grand escape from the country,
Or prove that I am, indeed, a functioning adult able to
    take care of myself.
Sadly my passport is out of date and I can barely walk a
    metre without the edges of the world turning dark and
    waking up with legs where my arms should be.
I would have liked to protest,
But it's hard to speak when your stomach is being crushed
    by an unnecessarily large piece of wood.
So I nod instead.
She said she'll be there on Tuesday to sit with me for
breakfast.
"It's my first day too, we'll be in it together."
I nod again, not because I want to, but because my neck
    no longer seems to be able to hold my head up for me.
She stands and the table gets slightly smaller again,

Enough that I can shuffle out and drag my feet across the carpet.
My shoes are scuffed and my socks don't stay up.
I'd like to lie down on the floor and sob for a moment, but
   I haven't been able to cry for months so it would look a
   little silly.
She has been talking this whole time but the words must
   have drowned on their way to me.
I do have a crumpled pile of sheets in my hand though.
They'll tell me where to go and how deeply they intend to bury me.

To be Needed

Collapsing,
fingers gripping cream bed sheets to feel something on
   the skin that isn't disdain.
Others crawl in here and I'm
unable to stop them.
I was never taught how to say no.

Instead,
I let myself be remoulded, repeatedly, into what people want.
I was going to say "need"
but that's entirely different.

Underneath it all I'm a heap of limbs that don't stand up straight
and they still want to take their hands and
their words to my shoulders and

Push.

I'd like to be taller, but I ache all over. Too late for that.

So,
I can't stand and
I can't sleep and
There's no in-between.
My knees touch my elbows and I melt into the mattress.

Travelodge 504

Away for the weekend.
I sit on starch sheets in a room too hot.
You can only open the window two inches and I think of
    the time a pair of bloodied scissors were hurled out of
    a similar window in the psych ward.
They lay rusted on the ground along with half a ball of
    orange yarn and it took them two
days to realise and do anything about it.
The outside, that is.
I dread to think what they did on the inside.

The lift smells like Disneyland pizza and I wonder how it
    would feel to spend the
evening in the liminal hotel space,
in all the places I hoped to run away to,
as all the versions of myself, since discarded.
The sea awaits though, along with the hundred faces I'll
    ignore, along with the hunger in my belly disguising
    itself as comfort again.

The last time I was here, a shooting star split the sky after
    I sucked you off on the beach
and it's strange to think that
even though neither of us exist anymore,
that moment is etched into the universe forever.

The Man in the Living Room

Jon Doyle

The planes were spraying again. That's what the man in
the living room said. He said, if you don't believe me,
stick your head out the window and look.

Richard's windows were painted shut so he stepped out
into the garden he shared with upstairs. A plastic table,
two stools, the sort of picnic bench they had outside pubs.
Upstairs didn't use the garden much because they were in
wheelchairs. The pair of them. Don't do drugs, the feller
had told him once, gesturing to where his legs had been.
Richard didn't ask what drugs had to do with it, but Mr.
Upstairs told him anyway. Something about abscesses.
The elusive search for a vein. Either way, they found it
difficult to get downstairs with no lift or anything. If they
ran out of shopping their daughter came over. If there was
a fire then God only knew.

It was warmer outside than in. Richard put his hand to

his forehead and squinted upwards. The man in the living room was right. Great sweeps of falling vapour dashed across the sky.

Mr. Upstairs called Richard "Russell", but it was too late to correct him now.

The planes flew from the near continent, the man in living room said when Richard went back inside. France, Germany, places like that. Didn't show up on the sky radars, of course. No finding them on flight logs.

You could track planes over the internet. Something Richard had learned from the man. You typed it into the computer and looked.

Well? the man said, eyebrows raised.

Richard leant against the doorjamb. Well what?

Well what are you going to do about it?

Richard hadn't planned on doing anything about it. What could he do about planes?

They're spraying in secret, the man said. Conducting experiments. Making subjects of us all.

Richard didn't remember inviting the man into his home. He'd been there a while now. Gave no indication of when he might leave. Richard offered him food and tea but his attention seemed enough for the man. As though an audience was the only thing any man could need.

The man sat with his hands in his lap. Barely seemed to be breathing. His face had a strangely indistinct quality, his features remaining unclear no matter how hard Richard looked.

You're going to want to wash it off, the man said.

Richard went through the kitchen and into the bathroom. He put the plug in the sink and set the tap to run. Was soap and warm water enough? He scrubbed his cuticles with the nail brush as he waited. When the sink was full, he added the faintest spritz of bleach.

You're going to have to do better than that, the man said from the living room. Those chemicals aggregate on fabrics and hair. You need to strip down, shave your head.

Richard stood in the doorway, palms stinging as though he had slapped something. As though his skin had been burned off and born anew.

The man in the living room understood about the chemicals because he'd read papers on them. Classified documents from military folks at Porton Down. He'd read a lot of papers, this man. He had sources all over the world.

Richard felt the heat flee his body as he took his jumper off. The coarse wool rough against his skin. He removed his shirt, his vest, the chain around his neck. His hands stinging and his face stinging and his eyes now stinging too.

The man in the living room watched as he undid the drawstring of his joggers. Mr. and Mrs. Upstairs wheeled around above their heads.

There are ways to protect yourself, the man said. Prophylactics you can take.

Back in the bathroom, Richard got the clippers from the medicine cabinet and plugged in the cord. Samantha used to cut his hair. She'd put a towel over his shoulders and work from right to left. Moving around in silence behind him, comb between her lips, occasionally bending his ears between her fingers so she didn't cut them off. Samantha wasn't rough exactly but she wasn't gentle either. She wasn't a professional, but she was functional and to the point. Always steering him straight, a single hand on the crown of his head, offering no complaint or rebuke no matter how many times he drifted.

The clippers sounded like a fly zapper on a chippie wall. The hair hit the sink in clumps. Richard leant low and pressed the blades tight to his scalp. The teeth left red furrows on the thin meat of his head. It hurt some but it didn't feel bad exactly. He wondered if Samantha cut the hair of whoever she lived with now.

The man in the living room was already talking when he returned. Something about the right to public goods. Something about a debt jubilee. Get your money out of the bank, he said calmly. Put your savings into silver, gold, decentralised currency.

Richard stood before him. A pale paper man in woollen socks and boxer shorts.

Can I get you something to eat?

The man in the living room didn't even shake his head.

It sounds like a good deal but it's not a good deal, he said. They want to make it so you never owned anything again.

In the kitchen, Richard prepared lunch. A slice of ham, two rounds of bread. A fuzzy growth in the corner but a bit of mould never hurt. The saying was Samantha's. A bit of mould never hurt. Wisdom passed down on her father's side. Repeated with such fondness you'd have thought she wanted the bread to have spoiled.

Richard looked at the slice again. Tiny bullseyes, up by the crust. Green-blue ringed with white.

A bit of mould never hurt. He heard it in Samantha's

voice.

Without feeling much of anything, he swept the plate to the ground.

Silence after the initial smash. Somehow boyish. The held breath of a guilty child. As though in remaining quiet the incident might pass by unnoticed. But who was going to notice now? Samantha wasn't there. His mother six feet underground. There was only the man in the living room, and he didn't care about such things.

He was still talking in there. Bouncing questions off the walls. On the floor, the ham spilled between the bread like a tongue. Richard searched the cupboards and found some tins. Soup. Cream of mushroom. Not his favourite flavour, but he had to eat something.

He opened the can, poured its contents into a pan and set the pan on the hob. He pushed the dial and turned. The hiss of gas. A panicked sound. A puncture in the world. He paused a moment, let the smell fill his nose.

Samantha had taken the stove lighter with her. Luckily there was a box of matches in the drawer. He struck one and waited a moment, letting the flame inch down towards his fingers, and then he lit the hob and blew out the match and went to throw the charred remains into the bin.

He almost slipped on the sandwich as he turned around. Sent shards of china skittering across the lino. The plate had been his mother's. Not one of her best plates but hers nonetheless. Her best plates were in a box under his bed, a complete set except for the one Samantha broke that Christmas, when they were all a lot younger and everyone was there.

What are you going to do about it? called the man in the living room.

Richard considered the shattered plate before him. Looked around for the dustpan and brush.

First they came for the sovereign citizens, the man in the living room said, but I did not care because I was not a sovereign citizen.

It took him a few moments to remember. The dustpan was out in the garden. He'd left it there after sweeping up the bottle someone had thrown over the wall. Kids were always breaking things around those parts. Found great joy in seeing one object become many in a flash.

The man in the living room eyed him as he re-entered. Quiet for the smallest moment. For once content to watch. Richard caught his own reflection as he went to the door. Bone-white and birdlike, head like a dead planet's minor moon.

The man said, surely you're not going out like that?

He had a plastic poncho in the cupboard. Army surplus, German flags on the arms. He had a pair of his father's steel-toed wellington boots. Gaffer tape, you need, the man said. Seal up the—, but Richard didn't stay to listen.

A wind moved low to the ground across the garden. Planes still spraying overhead.

The dustpan, the dustpan, he'd left it out there somewhere.

Russell, what 'appened to you?

Mr. Upstairs peered through the grill in front of the balcony French doors.

Samantha left, Richard called. She's living somewhere

else.

Mr. Upstairs's face dropped into shadow as he reversed a bit, straightened up and pulled forward again.

I wasn't talking about Samantha. I was on about your head.

Richard put his hand to his head gingerly, as though expecting to find something new there. The hood rustled like a paper bag.

Oh, he said. My head.

Look like one of them prisoners of war.

The wind blew against the poncho. Lifted it like a sail. Richard raised a hand in acknowledgement of the man and turned his back on him.

He lifted a sheet of tarpaulin. Checked behind the bins. They had a pond in the garden, empty now. Samantha had bought fish to put in there. Guppies, goldfish, miniature koi carp. They seemed happy until she got up one morning to find every single one had gone.

A heron, Samantha reckoned. These days, the pond was just a hole in the ground.

Richard got to his hands and knees, searching. Felt Mr Upstairs' eyes on the back of his head.

He found the pan beside the stack of shipping pallets Jimmy Jeffries had dropped off for him. Shipping pallets are always handy, that's what Jimmy said. People were always bringing him stuff after Samantha left. As though wishing to fill the gaps of the things she had taken, or else aware there was no-one left to stop them dumping stuff on him. Pallets, paint tins, the old frames of pull-out beds. Stuff it took three men to carry and drop into a pile.

The man in the living room was talking when he returned. Remember, he said, remember. It's never too late to act.

A sound from the kitchen like water running. Like wind whipping through a sea of flags.

His mind spasmed. The gas.

Smoke ghosted from beneath the door. Richard leant against the wood, felt the warmth against his face. The poncho tacky now, sticking to the panel as he shouldered through.

A seething thing before him. Consuming cabinets, curtains, the calendar on the wall. He took one step toward the heat and his boots sank into the viscous lino.

An unreal scene, slathered in grease. An acrid smell in his nose.

The soup amid everything, boiling on the countertop.

Forget about upstairs, the man in the living room said as Richard retreated and closed the door behind him. There's no use thinking of them now.

An alarm sounded as Richard backed against the far wall. Shrill screaming. Lizard brained. Activity upstairs. Frantic wheeling to and fro.

Smoke poured from beneath the door, tumbling upward like some backwards waterfall.

He heard shouting from upstairs. Richard standing there. Still in his poncho and boots.

Forget about them, the man repeated. They'd forget about you.

But he couldn't forget about them. Not while they yelled like that. He pushed out into the hall and up the adjoining stairs. Didn't even bother to knock.

There's a fire, he said. A fire. We've got to get you out.

Mr. and Mrs. Upstairs wheeled toward him, Mr. Upstairs pausing so his wife could go in front. Not a big woman by any stretch. Two men could get her down no problem at all.

Give me just a moment, Richard said. The entire plan suddenly clear.

Mrs. first, then Mr.

For two fit men it was no problem at all.

He took the stairs three at a time, the poncho sticking to his bare thighs, and he pushed into the living room to find the smoke billowing worse now, light flashing behind the door, and the alarm still screaming and the fire still screaming but the man in the living room was not in the living room anymore.

Nervosa

Ciaran Keys

I don't want to be judgemental or prejudiced, but I am. I just don't like some people. Or I need to hold them as examples of how "not like them" I am; use them to chase away the gnawing awareness that nothing concrete actually sets me apart from the perceived undesirables in my world. The feeling that as I'm walking behind them in the street, silently cursing how oblivious they are, someone is walking behind me doing exactly the same. I base my petty judgements on the ramshackle, shifting and ever self-serving list of Conclusions in my head; the few splinters of sense I can chisel from the world after years and years spent poking at my surroundings like loose teeth — instead of, say, learning anything or getting a job.

That's what I mean to convey, anyway. What comes out instead is a slurred spill of remarks regarding the people sitting across the carriage. A table of tense, quietly bickering men and women clustered around an old Nokia on their table as if it were about to split open and reveal the meaning of life. I mutter about how they probably think alcoholics are the real wasters. Nobody notices over B and F's outdoor-voice run-through of the jokes they've been repeating since school. They're sitting behind me, buffeting my seat as they fuck around and yell. Say what you want, I say to nobody in particular, the idea that they're lazy is bullshit. Never seen people who leg it around so much. Like message runners in the trenches. I must be staring, because a woman in a faded orange LaCoste jacket who could be 18 or 60 catches my eye. Lifts her chin and glowers. I redirect my gaze. I'm not trashed enough to start antagonising MOPs yet. The Nokia rings, reclaiming her attention and heading off the constructive discussion before it starts.

My friend D, a kind soul who I'll miss after I let him drift away, reaches past me and cracks a window. The night slaps me coldly in the face. It does that trick where the fresh air seems to kill your blood-alcohol ratio by about half and I focus on his face. He hands me another can.

"Reckon it's love, then?" he grins, cocking his head at the other table.

I glance back over at the woman in the orange hoody, who's biting her lip and staring out of the window as one of her mates whispers into the Nokia.

"No doubt. Eurgh."

The can he handed me is warm, but I gratefully suck about two-thirds of it down all the same. I'm at the "promises of Best Behaviour" stage of my nuisance-cycle so I stayed off the shorts tonight, and I'm feeling on edge.

"Where are we?"

"Just passed Fflint", he replies, laying his tobacco out on the table. "What's the plan after? I don't feel like going home yet."

"Mm. Might just go sit on the prom and have a smoke. They're pissing me off tonight."

Cracks have been showing in our little group for a while, actually. B and F are gearing up for greater things, killing time before they go to university. They've always liked the 'lads, lads, lads' rugby-guy image they have of themselves but lately they've been insufferable. I spend most of our conversations wishing they'd just lower their voices and back off a little bit. And B's nasty streak is widening; for a moment earlier tonight, I'd felt like slinging a bottle at him after yet another smirking putdown about my joblessness.

Something shifts across the carriage, an almost tangible wave of disappointment as Nokia man hangs up and says "nothing tonight now". His friends sit back in a quiet chorus of "fucksakes" and bitter sighs. Gutted, I think, before anxiously checking under the table that we still have more beers.

It's late when we get back, well after kicking-out time. Rhyl is always at its best in the early hours — the dark smooths out its decayed edges and the stragglers in evidence are usually too far gone to bother me. I half-heartedly try to talk the others into walking with me, grateful when they decline and head home. My shoulders tighten as I detour into the West End for the 24-hour

Premier. It's quiet but I always seem to sprout a "please give me a kicking" sign over my head down this end of town. The mumbling fixture behind the night hatch dispenses a half-bottle of Glenn's, which I uncap before he's finished counting out change. I sip urgently as I hurry to the seafront via John street, listening out for raised voices behind me.

The sea's out and I find a perch on a shredded groyne where the surf breaks apart. Light a crooked joint fished from my inside pocket and scroll through my tiny, outmoded mp3 player. I let my guard down and stare out at the wind farm's lighting arrays, remembering how I used to imagine the sound of their pulsing, thumping breath carried in on the wind.

With my brain lubricated and the right music turned loud, a sense of grounded reality settles over me. The individual moments of clattering, chromatic discord could be mistaken for roadworks or a faulty washing machine. But the way they twist and turn and cycle into one another seems to lend structure to the environment. Staccato micro-blasts of disharmony mutate pleasantly together into a whole, matching tempo with the slowly oscillating wavelets speckling my boots.

The evening replays itself, showing me which parts I was present for and which were my body slapping shoulders and lifting glasses while I sat inside, trying to formulate a way of signalling for help. It's freezing cold, but I don't mind. At intervals I startle and glance over my shoulder as though the town piled dimly behind me might be rearing up to bite. I don't want to be here; I don't particularly want to be anywhere else, either. The reality of where I'm headed encroaches and I respond in the only way I know how, by taking the boundless disappointment at who I'm becoming and turning it inside-out. Projecting it onto the town behind and the people in my life with such grandiose negativity that I can claim helplessness and postpone the exhausting climb ahead for another day.

In a small, modern country, each town exists only as a tangle. Knots in a dreamless, gangliate system woven from retail sprawl and thrown-up residency. They're considered separate entities by habit alone. Should any one fail outright it would be quickly picked away from the edges-in by its neighbours. No longer separate entities but thickenings, extrusions in a material swarming across its entire surface. A definable "end" no longer really factors into the existence of places like my home town, short of some disastrous glitch sufficient to poison or irradiate the soil. But rot they can, and do. The view from inside is a spoiling, heaving riot.

I grew up in a modern British town typical of its weight class and former occupation. In its early days, the majority were still reeling with dislocation at the rise and riptide pull of urbanised life on Earth. In their shock, they numbly accepted the picks and cotton-shuttles pressed into their hands on their way through the doors. What came into focus when their eyes adjusted to the gloom was unbearable, so outlets were required. As such, pleasure reserves were established along coastlines where the pit-weary and phosphorescently-jawed could gaze out to sea, or indulge in soothing 'pull lever, get trinket' behaviours of the most nakedly literal kind in flickering amusements parlours.

The model worked. A week's reprieve a year from the choking industrial waste aloft in the cities became the widely accepted payoff for lying across the moving gears of progress, as a footbridge for those yet unborn. It would have to be reward enough: even as those unlucky generations saw light at the end of the tunnel, the steel and steam geometry of their world was rearranging itself into a set of cantilevered jaws. The merciless, self-refining logic of industry snarled itself in what was left of tradition and tore both loose forever. The jaws snapped shut. The resultant war gouged enough from the population to set the resorts' downhill slide in progress, before its second half left the world so paradoxically rich and interconnected that the amusements at the end of the pier were forgotten to rust.

The world returned to its usual peacetime routine of constant arbitrary violence, but this time the sullen calm held. A seemingly inevitable third and final act of the war failed to commence. Our means of ending life had grown so obscenely efficient that we were shocked despite ourselves. The petrol fumes which filled the suddenly cramped space of the Earth finally persuaded even the feral strategists astride the Atlantic to take pause and stop lighting fires. Economies bloated beyond all reason in the pursuit of victory changed into civilian suits. The rivers of weaponry issuing from their mouths slowed, only to be dwarfed by oceans of consumer product. Barring proxy squabbles, tribal spats and corporate takeovers gone kinetic, the old approach to violence as control was no longer needed. In the new world everyone on the planet awoke to a gun in the face every single day by default, but soon most no longer saw it. The last Design for Life left standing after the quiet fell was one of eternal growth and ever more material comfort. In this climate of relative peace and plenty even a forgotten resort could live on the scraps. A reason to exist was no longer needed, as everywhere was joined together. Tourist towns with no tourists, cities built around industries sold overseas; all were placed on the life support of globalised commerce. If you ever look at your town and think, "why?", the answer lies in the echoing big-box retail parks planted like harvesters within convenient reach of its population.

It's around this point that my memory starts spooling. Allowing for rose-tinted glasses, the world seemed largely sane. The omnipresent media conveyed a general sense that everything was more or less moving forward.

Any child of a British town during those short years could count themselves lucky to have been born at that moment. To have experienced the instant the Design hung at the top of its parabolic arc and appeared permanent, whilst young enough to be fooled by the effect. If nothing else, they would be the last to be exposed to information at anything like a digestible rate. The new millennium wasted no time in souring the general air of optimism. Its first memories formed around a series of economic and social disasters, punctuated with unsettling spectacles of political violence calculated to ruin the mood. The effects of the internet on the human psyche resembled those of a brick tossed in a centrifuge. A queasy, unreal sensation set in as the rollercoaster of modernity inched into its vertical dive.

As an experiment, switch on the news. It will no doubt be less than cheerful. Let the usual feelings that everything must be falling apart tighten your chest for a moment. Then think about what exactly you are worried about. It can't simply be danger; only the chronically anxious assume they will be in the next plane to burst open in the sky, or plunged into starving poverty without warning. Empathy for those still limping along next to the rollercoaster waiting for their chance explains some of it, but we all have ruthlessly sophisticated mental blinders to temper that. Sensationalism and the tendency to focus on bloody spectacle share the blame, but are overrated. The quieter reports of dysfunction in the Design work away at us, too. The sick feeling that something has changed, that we are descending somehow, can't be based on any logical assessment of a set of problems; the world simply feels unhinged. Even the dullest B-roll footage behind news of a shortage in seasonal fruit is enough to bring on that nameless worry, viewed a certain way. A reminder of how precarious everything might really be, a clog in the great feeding tube. The world a nightmare of icons, logos, arrows, advertising, plastered across every surface, all designed to seize attention and impart the most information possible. Pointless rituals of forlorn yellow hazard tape and awareness-raising lectures, with no more power to shield us from misfortune's flailing hammer than a rabbit's foot.

Fixed expressions of sincere optimism atop colour-coded ties asserting that all is under control, believed by nobody but the conspiracy junkies sworn to doubt them.

To be raised in this context, even defective and barely clinging on, is still to enjoy comforts unimagined by the people who first holidayed at the forgotten resorts. To complain might be a total spitting-upon of all they sacrificed to get us here. But something is beginning to give. The herd grows ever more neurotic and restless, well-fed or not. With the world a giant, flickering amusements parlour we frantically pull levers and despair that only trinkets come out.

In the clutch of short years since my friends went on ahead, my collapse has become a freefall. The population of the Earth has dwindled to a handful, befitting the two small Welsh towns and intervening railway that encompass what remains of the planet. I don't really see it anymore.

Sometimes I try to feel that old soothing antipathy again. Probe for the hostile tension that used to give me a boundary between what was inside and what was outside in lieu of a functioning sense of self. Nothing.

Walking uphill makes me sweat and fear that the figures moving past will scent the weeks of caked-in neglect sealed beneath my coat. Getting on the train means noise and swaying. Getting off means more walking until I can be back at my desk, buried away from the unbearable chaos of quiet side streets and the occasional car. I connect with my surroundings to the same extent as do larvae on a branch shying away from sudden heat or cold.

About half the people in the world work split shifts at the 24-hour shop down the street. The other half, my tiny precious family and remaining friend, live beyond the rattling torment of the forty minute train ride to Rhyl. Once a week I go there to spend the afternoon dutifully standing upright and maintaining eye contact with my family so as not to leave them feeling totally abandoned. Soon my son will be old enough to question my bizarrely stilted presence and I won't know what to tell him.

My mum buys us lunch. The worry in her eyes is so long-ingrained it no longer jars when she smiles and comments on how lovely it is to see us both. Then I go to J's and slam shut the window of encroaching sobriety. He drinks too, because I'll hassle and whine if he doesn't. He sits bundled with tension and half turned away, playing videogames and curtly affirming my repetitive, looping diatribes. As the night wears on he occasionally pauses and turns to regard me with naked disdain as I dredge up the worst of the mental slurry I've accumulated since we last spoke. Sometimes there's enough of me still functioning socially to be offended, and I start a bitter row that I'll try to piece together on the train ride home in the morning from the scraps I can recall. J is the only person on earth I can talk to. I can tell it won't be long before his door is closed to me altogether. I do this every week all the same.

Mostly, though, it's just me and the flat. I cannot understand how I am still being allowed to live here. They know what I've done to it; I stopped answering the door or replying to phone calls, so the repairman simply lets himself in when boiler access is required. The rental agent occasionally comes and stares disbelievingly about while I shove shopping bags of broken glass in corners and describe my plans to catch up on the arrears.

Since the last of my personality boiled away in night sweat I seem to have acquired a protective aura against outside interference. People just want to be away from it all. It feels as though I could hold out the money I owe and they'd insist I keep it, unwilling to touch anything I'd touched. Footsteps down the concrete stairs outside no longer induce panic, because I know nothing will ever change. I'm in catastrophic debt and yet the lights stay on. Once a fortnight the state dumps money into my account. I cycle between the desk and the bed at days-long intervals. Come around in the dark totally bewildered as to whether I've just ended a binge or if I've been lying poisoned so long there'll be radio chatter and hi-viz at the front door soon, taking a deep breath before giving the nod to force the lock.

I keep flicking all the old switches but nothing can rouse the inert block pressing drily against the inside of my skull. All the stand-bys have worn thin with long exposure. Confirming, yet again, that my ex has scrubbed all trace of me from her online presence and severed all contact leaves me with a dull ache where there used to be jaw-clenching, galvanising grief. The songs that instantly launched me up or smashed me down on demand finish before I've heard them.

Reading about life's endless serialised soap opera no longer triggers grandiose moments of understanding; only a creeping guilt that I should dare feel anything but gratitude as I sit in safety drinking my government handouts. Commemorated forever in glory or dying faceless and bathed in radiation, the people on those pages are as distant as dust belts behind the stars.

I'd give anything for one more night of maudlin histrionics and spikes of defiant optimism. But nothing can unclog the conduit to myself. Nothing induces those sudden manic resolves to turn over a new leaf, or outbursts of tearful sympathy towards myself and everyone else and the whole sorry mess.

I get one brief reprieve. For no reason that I could ever pinpoint, there is a night where it all switches back on for a few joyous, intolerable moments. I awake as usual coiled around my cramping stomach, suffocating in damp sheets and panic that the blackness in my window means everything's finally disappeared for good. I eventually make it from bed to desk and root out a warm plastic half-bottle of black rum. As I begin sipping and gagging I cue up some music on my laptop, a good song but not one that ever affected me before. Then it has me and I'm breathing raggedly, meeting my own staring eyes in the window. A jolt of sheer experience pins me that way until the sky begins to silver outside, and then it's gone.

Had I known then it would be the last time, and that it would be years yet before I could leave the flat and get sober, I think I might have simply switched off. My body would have wound down like a clock until it slumped in the gap between bed and desk, pupils unresponsive to the dawn.

I learn later that mystical experiences are quite common in people detoxing from alcohol, which is reassuring and disappointing in equal measure. Right now, though, the stained-glass significance of everything has me in full sway and I regard M the liaison nurse like some sort of angel. She's fighting for me, trying to tell them all the things I can't say. The psychiatrist taps his pen on the desk as she speaks. When he responds, he sounds as though he's deciding on where to put an item of furniture.

"No history of suicidal attempts, apparently titrating quite well with home visits. I can't justify filling a bed."

My history *is* a suicidal attempt, I think, looking from his face to hers and back. Ever patient, M reiterates on my behalf:

"I'm concerned about Ciaran's memory. He's having trouble counting doses and his withdrawals are worsening. I don't believe a home detox is safe."

It's a weird punchline to twenty years of refusing to quit; now that I desperately want to, I can't. I have to taper off, riding the line daily between too much and not enough. I've been trying to tell them for weeks I can't stomach another drop, that it's impossible to keep track when my memory won't hold anything. I try again, raising my hand like a schoolchild and attempting to speak. The psychiatrist makes eye contact for the first time and shushes me.

I'm too drained to be angry. I know how the game works. I saw it enough times growing up. To be heard I'd have to kick and swear, draw down the police and become too much trouble to ignore. I just can't do it. I've programmed myself to appear quiet and orderly for too long. I'm going to die of politeness.

"…and the wisdom to know the difference."
It's a good system, if you know its limits. The guys who

developed the AA programme were absolute space cadets. Doesn't mention that part in the book, obviously, but the psychedelics they dabbled in shine through. That quasi-religious glow when you first get sober is a powerful tool in the right hands, gives you a foothold to start climbing out of the Skinner box and acting like a sentient being. And I like my sponsor. We baffle each other frequently but his days in the box sound a lot like mine, and I'm reassured by the calm way he carries himself. I get as much out of his neat haircut and always-clean glasses as his words.

One year. The glow is gone and my inner monologue is growing harsh again. I have long stretches of dysfunction, scuttling the big plans I've made. But I don't fall. I see others forgetting how it ended and going back into oblivion. Some come back. Most don't. The fact that I'm allowed to drive a car regularly stuns me. I find a job that requires constant, enthusiastic interaction with strangers and it fits somehow.

Three years. I've outgrown the halfway-house community I moved to after leaving the flat. I try to contribute but I've heard the slogans a million times too many and start to think of moving on. Another escapee from the box arrives and hits my life like a burning blessed comet. She is at no risk of dying from well-behaved politeness and soon we're out on our own with doors slammed shut behind us. I take a picture of her looking out to sea on a sunny day at Porth Wen brickworks, and realise my course is absolutely set.

Five years. We've just moved to a city. I sit in traffic, surrounded by all the things I've always feared and find myself quite enjoying it. On such a scale the kaleidoscope of people, warning signs and architecture makes a kind of sense. It's so dense and crowded it goes all the way around to feeling pleasantly lonely again.

We still have a long way to go. We've harnessed our ravenous brains with small, relatively harmless vices but life is often hard. The injuries we incurred throwing ourselves at walls all those years still pain us. We're still children, really, picking up at the point where we first fell through the cracks. But we have a chance. Tonight I'll sit in my garden listening to the sirens in the distance and breathe out, knowing the first leg of the climb is done.

Darkness Brighter than the Sun

Amy Kitcher

"The coffin, the casket, whatever. We need a bigger one, right?" The words disappear down the crackling phone line. Orange-patterned walls creep closer. The tiny front room hasn't seen a paintbrush since the seventies and it stinks of stale baccy.

"...only five-feet tall."

"What?"

"He was five-feet tall, JJ. Seems a waste to spend more than necessary."

Fuck you, Malcolm. The edge of my vision shimmers red. Grandad towered. Had towered. A giant amongst men. A colossus. Yes, okay, I matched him height-for-height at twelve. And later I grew taller. But he had stature. No one beat Grandad for stature. Especially not fucking Malcolm the Miser. "Why not get a cardboard one, then? Or better still, just leave him outside to rot?"

"Grow up. Look, have you decided what you're doing yet?"

"No."

"Well, make up your mind soon because we need to sell the house." The line goes dead.

I want to smash the damn phone. Smash fucking Malcolm, too. But the only pleasure I have these days is confounding their expectations, so I replace the brown plastic receiver in its cradle as gently as a newborn baby. Tea. I need tea. A splash of scotch. Or two. I take my medicine and head into the garden.

Towards the shed.

Head down. Watching one foot and a clumsy, metal-filled shoe negotiate the gauntlet of stepping stones, avoiding any glimpse of the borders, crammed with obscenely cheerful flowers. I close my eyes as I pass the flattened patch where he fell. An ugly temptation spawned when I heard the news. *Take a hedge trimmer — a flamethrower! — to the bloody lot*, it whispered. But I didn't. The day he retired, Grandad traded his pickaxe for a spade. Swapped the eternal night of the coal mine for the vivid days of his garden. He'd never have forgiven me for declaring war on his flower beds.

White confetti from the cherry blossom dusts my chest and shoulders and I brush off the petals with an impatient hand. The bastard tree weeps more easily than me.

I turn the final bend. There. The shed, basking like a cat in a slice of sun. I can't remember when the clapboards looked less than freshly painted, or a cascade of blooms didn't grace the window box he'd constructed from a discarded wooden pallet. In the deepest winter, with snow up to your knees, Grandad coaxed something to grow. Heather maybe, or a clump of hot-pink cyclamen.

I pull open the door and duck under the doorframe.

Cross the threshold of an old man's shed and you cross a border into a foreign land. Each has unique customs, laws and anthems. Grandad would give The Nod before anyone set foot inside. The offer and acceptance of tea would follow, with all the ritual of a Japanese ceremony. The biscuit tin appeared as if by magic. Inspection of seed catalogues and the complex planning and placement of communal bulk orders took place in the dark months. Any family milestone, an engagement, a birth, an exam result, merited a toast with hedgerow homebrew. University graduation — the most hallowed achievement — earned the hip flask. A demijohn of elderberry wine probably lingers in the cupboard, wrapped in a moth-eaten bodywarmer and tied up with twine. I can't bring myself to check.

The place is warm, stuffy almost. The thick air shimmers with smells of sawn wood, hot dust and four-stroke oil. Grandad's own scent. I lift a deckchair from a hook, flick it open one-handed and slump down. The old boards creak beneath my weight. The shed looks the same. To my right, a menagerie of jam jars filled with nails, screws, nuts, bolts, washers. To my left, toolboxes stacked corner-straight, filled with initial-scratched spanners of every size, hickory-handled hammers, wicked sharp saws, oil cans, mallets. The obligatory scarred workbench. A shelf of half empty paint tins. Yellow newspapers thriftily stored to make biodegradable pots for seedlings. A tidier man than Grandad you'll never meet. Everything had its place. Even the spiders kept their webs all neat and Disney-fied for him. Not a single mousetrap, either. Vermin wouldn't dare enter Grandad's domain, let alone steal grass seed or bird food.

I toe the faded jute rug running the length of the shed. Keeps the cold from rising, Grandad said. One corner of the rug curls up like an autumn leaf, coaxed out of shape by the passage of his feet over the years.

I drain the tepid dregs of tea and put the cup on the floor. The whisky hasn't thawed the ice block in my stomach. Doesn't touch the dependency that lurks in my marrow.

Half an hour. Nip into town. Score a hit.

Piss off!

I rip back the rug. A cloud of dust mushrooms into the air. No gaping mouth. No hungry, black-throated monster. Just a trapdoor, hasp neatly set in a chiselled-out bed. The hinges don't creak, they never have. But even Grandad failed to impose his iron will on the damp grave-stench that wafts from the cavity.

Four straight walls, each two foot six inches. At the bottom, off at a right angle, a horizontal chamber. Originally five-feet long, later Grandad enlarged it to six. A place to lay when tiredness delivered a knockout punch. The Demon Hole, we called it. Yes, everything had its place in Grandad's shed.

Even me.

The foetid draught trails an icy finger across the exposed skin at my wrists and neck. I suppress a shiver as I lower myself to the floor, swing my legs over, and drop inside. The trapdoor thunks closed above me. Different degrees of darkness exist, measured — in simple terms — by the absence of light. The darkest places have never felt the sun, have no knowledge, no memory, of our blinding fireball.

Darker and colder, to the power of ten, the depths of The Demon Hole.

Panic ignites, flares tracer-bright in my chest. The fingernail-ripping scramble. Skull-searing pain. The lash of unsatisfied cravings. Remembered sensations echo inside me and I bump off the walls like a grenade down a drain pipe.

How long did I spend down here? A week? A fortnight? Longer? Pissing in a pop bottle. Leaking diarrhoea. Sleeping on the wet earth, a woollen blanket between me and the worms. Surfing wave after wave of hallucination. Hearing scratching and breathing. Groping for my absent leg, finding a phantom limb alive with maggots. Seeing glutinous corpses root through the soil. Fighting my demons, Grandad called it. I won the battle, I suppose.

Grandad didn't. He never outran his demons. Yeah, he'd get a furlong ahead now and again, but they always caught him in the end. And when they clawed him, gnawed at him, twisted him so bad he couldn't sleep without screaming, he put himself in the hole. Faced them down. Again. And again.

He never spoke about his role in the War. Men didn't back then. I guess we don't now either. I certainly never talk about that last patrol in Chah-e Anjir and the man I caught beating a crippled girl. Or about the twenty-one days in-service detention I got for intervening. Or how it had all been a distraction so the Taliban could ambush us. How three of the best mates I'll ever have begged to be shot at the end.

Half an hour. Nip into town. Score a hit.

PISS OFF!

As a kid, Grandad's service record was a jigsaw puzzle for me to solve. I thought myself so damn clever, piecing it together. Like Sherlock Holmes, or Hercule Poirot. And like a famous detective, I did the big reveal in front of the whole family in the tiny orange front room.

"You dug six miles of tunnels and detonated nineteen mines and killed ten thousand Germans! People heard the explosion in London. The crater is four-hundred and twenty-three feet —"

"Stop it, Johnny," Grandad said and stood up and left the room. He was a hero. Why did he look so sad, I wondered?

Silence arrived that day, took up residence, filled every crevice it could find. Talking about feelings, discussing concepts like love, honour and forgiveness? Luxuries belonging to the middle class. Not us.

At sixteen, my father told me: you work. You don't complain. He forgot the last part: you die. And your family argue how much the funeral will cost.

Two decades after I outed Grandad, I returned from Afghanistan dead on the inside, with half a leg and a heroin addiction. I only felt alive in a country I hated, doing a job that could kill me. My family were ghosts. Or maybe I was the ghost, I couldn't tell. Grandad turned up unannounced at the MDHU where I was festering.

After taking four buses and a cross-country train to get there, he marched in and began ordering me about like the sergeant he'd been. Our lives collided and the past was obliterated. He offered the only medicine he possessed and when we got home, he locked me in the dark beneath the shed — bed sores and all — and his love shone brighter than the sun. No words required.

I clamber out of the hole, check my prosthesis hasn't come loose and shut the trap door. It doesn't matter what size, what material, they choose for Grandad's casket. He won't suffer it for long. Three hours or so, for the service and cremation. Afterwards, he'll soar on the wind and never have to lay under the cold heavy earth ever again.

Danny in the Dragon's Den

Simone Greenwood

Danny Mabbett has an ENORMOUS PROBLEM ... there's a dragon living in Grandpa's cellar and it's eaten his parents ... and his new friend's head.

Extract from children's book *Danny in the Dragon's Den* by Simone Greenwood, who thankfully only had a few toads living in her cellar when she was Danny's age.

Chapter 1: Too Much Death

The feeling Danny Mabbett feels most often is hunger.

The feeling he feels second most often is missing his parents, but the hunger growls louder and so it gets top spot.

I know that lots of stories start with a child whose parents have sadly died, and you might be thinking ENOUGH ALREADY WITH ALL THE PARENTS DYING, but nothing else would happen the way it does if they had stayed alive, so you would be reading another book entirely. You might decide to do that anyway, which is totally fine (read whatever you like) but there's a headless chicken coming up called Bobina and it would be a shame to miss her.

Grandpa often feels hungry too, mostly because he forgets to buy food and forgets to cook. But he also forgets he's hungry, which is just as well. That's why Danny's parents decided to move in with Grandpa in his big old house; so they could look after him. It was the first time they'd been to visit since he'd moved to the seaside after Nan died.

Sorry. Another death. I can only apologise for all the dying. Brace yourself, there's more coming.

Chapter 2: Unprecedented

Danny's story starts right slap bang in the middle of a global pandemic. You probably know what one of those is, and what it feels like living through one, but if you're reading this underwater in the Year 3000, or have been living in a cave and this is the first time you've ventured out in a while, here's a quick explanation:

A global pandemic is when a virus spreads around the world (that's the global bit) and makes lots of people sick (that's the pandemic bit) and to try and stop the virus where Danny lived, the government told everyone to stay inside their houses or flats or caravans and to keep away from everyone else. Most children had to do their school lessons at home, and could only go outside to play if they had their own garden, which of course not every child does.

Adults also had to work from home, unless they were a key worker (which actually had nothing to do with keys) or wrestled crocodiles for a living (crocodiles do not like to be wrestled indoors). Normal life was anything but normal. People used the word UNPRECEDENTED until it didn't mean what they thought it meant anymore.

This story is not about a virus though. It's about Danny, and what happened to his parents ... and what happened next. Danny's mam and dad didn't die because of a virus. They died because of the dragon in the cellar. Who ate them. And a few days later he burped up some bones. It was actually pretty gross, and of course very upsetting, including for the dragon who got indigestion and felt sorry for himself.

Let's start at the beginning, on the very day Danny and his parents arrived with all their suitcases and boxes at Grandpa's clifftop house by the sea. After all the effort of lumping and bumping their belongings inside, they fancied a cup of tea and a biscuit. Actually, Danny would have preferred orange juice but he loved a tea-dunked biscuit, even though he was still mastering his technique. Sometimes he'd have to scoop out soggy-dropped-off-bits with a teaspoon.

Grandpa's kitchen was a bit dirty and smelly, so Mrs Mabbett went to wash up some mugs only to find there was no hot water. She declared that the boiler must be on the blink, and fetched her tool box to go take a look in the cellar ... where the boiler was ... and also something else. If you've been paying attention, you'll know exactly what else was in the cellar when she headed down the steps with a cheery Won't be long! and why she never came back.

Upstairs, they heard some strange might-not-be-the-boiler noises, and Mr Mabbett shouted down, "HONEY ARE YOU OKAY?" at least three times before he went to see what was happening. He never came back either.

Danny waited and waited and waited. He looked out the kitchen window and watched a seagull doing a tap dance (seagulls are very good at tap dancing) and listened to more strange noises coming from the bottom of the cellar steps. By this point, he was feeling both bored and nervous, so asked Grandpa if they should go and see what was happening together. Grandpa stared blankly ahead. Then little sparks flickered in his eyes, as if he'd suddenly remembered something very, very important (which he had). "DON'T GO IN THE CELLAR, THERE'S A DRAGON DOWN THERE!" he bellowed, but it was far too late and Danny knew it.

The sound and smell of a loud burp floated up to the kitchen and Danny gulped, then slammed the cellar door shut. He turned the key, pulled it out, and held it so tight in his hand it dug into his skin. Grandpa whispered, "Purple pumpkins!" and slowly crossed his chest, then forgot about the whole thing and shuffled off to watch *Escape to the Seaside* on the telly.

Danny glared after him. "THIS IS ALL YOUR FAULT, GRANDPA!" he yelled, but there was no reply. He slumped into a chair and stared at the key in his hand. Then he cried until snot came out of his nose, which happens when you cry a lot. He stared and cried and wiped snot and tears from his face until his hands and the key were all one big blodgy snotty blur.

At last, when he'd run out of tears and snot, Danny got up and looked round for a place to hide the key. He wasn't even sure why he needed to hide it, but it seemed like the right thing to do. He decided to slide it underneath the tick-tocking brass clock on the shelf above the fireplace; in the gap between the clock's four ball-shaped feet.

Grandpa laughed at something on the telly in the front room, and Danny hated him for it. He hated him until his body shook with hate. But then he thought about his lovely parents, and realised he could hate Grandpa as much as he hated pickles or sprouts, but it would never make them uneaten.

"He didn't forget on purpose," Danny said out loud. "And he's all the people I've got now … it's just me and him."

He felt a little better for deciding not to hate Grandpa, but that didn't stop him from having a BIG problem ... an UNPRECEDENTED problem ... perhaps the most ENORMOUS PROBLEM in the whole wide world.

Chapter 3: The Last Chicken

Danny's ENORMOUS PROBLEM recap:

He was stuck in a new-to-him house, in a new-to-him town, with Grandpa to look after and a dragon living in the cellar ... who had just eaten his parents! He couldn't even go and knock at the house next door to ask for help because he didn't know them AND there was a global pandemic. Besides, he was pretty certain that if he did tell anybody about what had happened, sooner or later Grandpa would be put in a home for forgetful grandparents ... and he wasn't even sure where they'd put him. And what about the dragon? If he told anyone about *that*, they probably wouldn't believe him and wander down into the cellar to prove it was all in his imagination ... and then they'd get eaten too.

If that makes you feel sad, just imagine how sad Danny felt, because it actually happened to him; he didn't read about it in this book. If it doesn't make you even the tiniest bit sad, then my guess is *YOU* are the parent-eating dragon or one of his dragon mates, in which case kindly stop reading and go and think about what you've done. Go on. Put the book down and go.

Thankfully, for all you non-dragons left, I have some good news ... because the very next day Danny found a friend. This friend couldn't help with his ENORMOUS PROBLEM, but sometimes having a friend beside you is all you need to feel a little better about whatever it is you are facing.

Let's start at the moment Danny woke up. His belly was rumbling and gurgling and that's when he remembered he hadn't eaten anything for ages because no one had been there to cook for him. Grandpa had been there, but as you know, he was too forgetful to cook for himself or anyone else.

When Danny went downstairs to hunt in the kitchen for something to eat, he noticed half a packet of biscuits on the kitchen table ... the ones they all would have happily dunked into mugs of tea yesterday if it wasn't for the ENORMOUS PROBLEM. He gobbled every last crumb and then felt guilty for not offering Grandpa at least one of the biscuits, but he wasn't even sure where Grandpa was.

He checked the front room, and Grandpa's bedroom, but there was no sign of the old man anywhere in the house. He went back to the kitchen and looked at the door to the cellar and shuddered, then hurried to check if the key was still under the clock. It was, and when he tried the cellar door handle, it was still locked shut, so Grandpa couldn't be down there.

But what if there was another key somewhere and Grandpa forgot about the dragon again? To be safe, he fetched a felt tip pen from a box labelled *Danny's Things* and wrote *NO ENTRY* in big capital letters on the door. Underneath he drew his best attempt at an angry dragon, then underneath that he wrote *DEADLY!!!!!*

At least there was one thing he didn't have to worry about, which was the dragon getting up the cellar steps and into the house. His reason for not worrying about that was because Grandpa had been living in the house by the sea for months and months, and was (so far) uneaten.

Then Danny felt a sea breeze coming in through the back door, and realised it was a tiny bit open. He wondered if Grandpa had gone outside to the garden so went to check. He found him in the shed, staring into a large cardboard box. The cardboard box was wiggling.

"Purple pumpkins," muttered Grandpa. "It's still alive!"

"What's still alive?" asked Danny, and Grandpa jumped.

"Who are you? Get out of my shed!"

"It's me, Grandpa ... Danny."

Grandpa shrugged and pointed into the box.

"The last chicken!"

Chapter 4: Bobina

Now take a deep breath, because this is going to seem super impossible, but I want to reassure you that (in this chapter at least) nobody dies.

Inside the cardboard box, inside the shed, inside the garden of the clifftop house by the sea was a ... headless chicken.

Yes, that's right, a chicken with no head.

There was a bit of a neck, with feathers partly covering a hole that Danny pretended was smeared in ketchup and not any other kind of red substance, and the rest of the chicken was all exactly as it should be; gingery-brown, fluffed-up feathers, two flapping wings, two scrawny legs and two clawed feet. And those feet were pacing back and forth.

"What happened?" asked Danny, feeling discombobulated; which is a fancy way of saying confused and a bit freaked out.

"I dunno, lad," Grandpa shrugged.

"You said it was the last chicken. What happened to the other chickens?" quizzed Danny, like a reporter from the local newspaper. He wished he could borrow his dad's phone to take a video of the flapping, headless bird, but he couldn't, because both his dad and the phone were in the belly of a dragon. Danny knew this because ninety-nine percent of the time his dad's phone was either in his dad's hand or in his dad's pocket.

Danny looked properly around the shed for the first time, and noticed a chicken coop at one end and some large bags with *Alexander Matthew's Super Duper Chicken Feed* written on them. Clearly, Grandpa had been keeping lots of chickens. There was plenty of smelly poo as evidence too.

"I don't know how it got in this box. Maybe I put it there? I've never had one escape half eaten before," said Grandpa, forgetting to answer Danny's question but remembering to scratch his head. "Best I get it out and send it back down to Orcibus straight away. He'll be mighty miffed!"

The old man bent down to scoop up the headless chicken but Danny instinctively got in the way to stop him.

"Wait, who's Orcibus?" he asked, fairly sure he knew exactly who Orcibus was. But Grandpa started to whistle a tune and then asked about the weather.

"It's getting a bit drizzly, Grandpa," said Danny, trying his best not to get frazzled. When his mam got frazzled, she always said it was time for a cup of tea, so Danny suggested they both go back inside and he'd put the kettle on. "I'm not sure I'm old enough to be boiling a kettle though," he added, but things felt very different since the ENORMOUS PROBLEM, so he figured new rules would have to apply.

"Don't be daft lad, your dad will make us a cuppa. He makes lovely eggs and bacon too. Is he up yet? What about your mam?"

Danny had no idea how to answer Grandpa's questions, but thankfully, he was already wandering off back towards the house, still whistling. Danny followed, but turned back for one last look at the pacing chicken.

It was an equally horrible and awesome sight, and in that moment, he knew he couldn't leave the wretched bird to its fate alone. It was too late to save his parents, but he could at least try to help this hopeless, headless creature; even if all he could do was put the box in the house for a bit of warmth. He thought having no head probably meant you were more likely to catch a chill.

He hurried back towards the house, trying to see over the top of the cardboard box and not trip on the various bits of junk lying about in the overgrown grass. The drizzle had turned to rain, and fat blobs were landing on his face. Ahead, Grandpa was already closing the kitchen door and might have locked it shut if Danny hadn't shouted out, "WAIT FOR ME!"

As he rushed safely inside, Danny noticed a curtain moving in an upstairs window in the house next door, and a half-hidden face looking down at him. But he was too busy thinking about the headless chicken to pay much attention.

"I'll call you Bob," said Danny, placing the box down on the kitchen floor next to the unlit fireplace. The feathery body wiggled a bit, and a brown egg fell out and rolled around.

"Oh ... you're a girl chicken. In that case, I'll call you Bobina."

Chapter 5: One Egg, No Bacon

Danny watched as Bobina's egg popped and sizzled in the frying pan. He'd looked in the fridge for some bacon, or anything else that would go with it, but there was nothing but a squidgy cucumber and a jar of disgusting-looking pickles.

He wondered how he'd make one egg fill two grumbling tummies; he could hear Grandpa's, and could feel his own, despite the gobbled biscuits. It wasn't a nice noise or a nice feeling, but the sizzling sounded good.

Happily, there was some milk in the fridge door, so he made them both a cup of tea. He'd only half boiled the kettle though, because he didn't dare let it fully boil on his first attempt.

When the egg was done, he scooped it out from the pan with a spatula and slid it onto a plate, then carefully cut it in half and slid one side onto another plate. There were bits of broken egg shell in it, but he was proud of his first attempt at cooking.

"Where's the bacon? What about the toast? You've forgotten the brown sauce," complained Grandpa when Danny put a plate in front of him. "And why is this tea lukewarm? Yuck!"

Danny felt like blurting back some angry questions of his own, like *Why are you feeding a dragon in your cellar when you can't feed yourself?* and *Why are you so ungrateful when I've tried my best?* Plus some not angry ones like *Who's Luke Warm?* and *How long can a headless chicken survive?* But instead, he just huffed a bit and went to look in the pantry cupboard to see what else he could find.

There was a pack of cream crackers, a few tins, and a couple of wrinkly apples. That was it.

He shut the cupboard and sat down at the table feeling miserable. Grandpa had already finished both egg halves and was licking one of the plates.

"Grandpa, we need more food!"

"Your mam will go shopping when she's up."

"No Grandpa … she's … never mind."

"Getting a bit nippy lad, pop the heating on."

"The boiler's broken, we need to light the fire … for us and for Bobina."

The old man looked up, and a bit of runny yolk ran down his stubbly chin. "Bobina? Who's that?"

Danny looked over at the cardboard box on the floor, and realised it was best not to draw Grandpa's attention to her. "Erm … why don't you go in the front room and watch telly, Grandpa?" he said.

Grandpa seemed pleased with the idea and shuffled out into the hall. A few moments later Danny heard the sound of the TV blaring out something about hammers and homes.

Another sound – a scratching one – came from the cardboard box to remind him that Bobina was MIRACULOUSLY STILL ALIVE! He sat down beside the box, on the cold and dirty floor, and realised he wasn't the only one with an ENORMOUS PROBLEM.

"Looks like we're both having a terrible time," said Danny. "I imagine having no head feels as horrible as having no parents and no food." Bobina would probably have clucked something back if she'd still had her beak.

"Don't worry, we'll figure something out," he said, patting her feathery back, but making sure not to touch anywhere near her neck because it looked super grim and a bit oozy. "It's not like things could get any worse!"

Perhaps it would've been best for Danny not to say the last bit out loud, because, at that very second, some soot scattered down the chimney and made both of them jump. Then the tiled floor underneath them began to shake, and the cold tea left on the table wobbled about and spilled over. Bobina paced back and forth in her box in alarm, and Danny was feeling pretty alarmed himself; especially when the cellar door handle rattled and the whole kitchen felt like an earthquake had hit. But the most alarming thing of all was the noise that boomed from below. It was deep and growly and sounded very much like the words *FEED ME*.

(un)common

The Changing Room

Bridget Keehan

I've nicked stuff before and got away with it: a small
compact of silver dream eye shadow from Boots, which
slipped up my sleeve, and a silver bangle engraved with a
tiny heart that I tried on then "forgot" to take off. These
little steals usually happen with my best mate, Murph,
who doesn't need to nick stuff because her parents buy
her whatever she wants. She just does it for a laugh. I love
her but she can be a liability in a shoplifting situation.
Unlike me she doesn't blend easily into the background.
She's model tall, but not model skinny, and never steps
out the door without her bright red lipstick and big hoop
earrings. Compared to her I'm the quiet one. I blush easy
and although I try to look people in the eye, in case they
think I'm lying, I'd much rather focus on their chin.

When Dad asks how I'm going to earn a living when
I leave home, and I tell him that I'm going to be an

actress, I get why he laughs. He's not one for taking things seriously. Except money, he takes that very seriously.

"There's no money in acting Aisling, you'll end up a sponger."

"What's a sponger?"

"A money leech. A parasite. *Never a lender or a borrower be*. Or if you do borrow make sure it's off a bank and you never pay it back."

Dad has a talent for making money, and for remembering lines from Shakespeare, but he's not like other people's dads who sweat their lives away on building sites or do boring office work. Losers, he calls them, wage slaves who waste their time doing what toffs tell them to. Like him I want to be rich, but I'm not sure I'm cut out to be a crook. There's a part of me that is more like Mam and would rather keep my head down. Take shoplifting; it doesn't come easy to me but at least I know how you go about it, whereas becoming an actress, well that's a mystery.

So here I am in town on a Saturday afternoon, clutching a plastic Faircost supermarket bag in one hand and my small beaded purse in the other. The purse is an embarrassment. It looks like a child's. Inside is a scrunched fiver, my cash-in-hand wage from my morning's work of making beds and cleaning bogs at the Majestic Hotel, which is anything but. I know five quid will, at best, buy me a trendy t-shirt from Chelsea Girl, but I don't intend to spend it, unless of course I bottle it. Nerves can sometimes get the better of me.

Entering the shop I clock an assistant at the till who barely acknowledges me as I head to the rails of swish new shirts. Quickly I find the one for me: black check and sleeveless. I notice another sales assistant to my left, rearranging a rack of jeans. I wander over, select the style I'm after, and shyly ask if I can try them on along with the shirt. She smiles, a Debbie Harry dazzler, and leads me upstairs to the changing rooms, shiny bangles jangling around her wrists.

In the Chelsea Girl changing room I stare at my reflection in the mirror and for once I like what I see. My hair, recently bleached to look more like Murph's, matches my new, cool outfit. I finger the soft denim and turn to check myself from a side-on angle. The shirt goes so well with the grey jeans. Grandmaster Flash and the Furious Five are pumping "The Message" through the shop's speakers and I dance to the music within the confines of the cubicle, trying to shake off the nerves fluttering in my gut. Dad's voice in my head reminding me, *only stupid crooks get caught.*

Most of his misdemeanours have gone undetected and, on the rare occasions he has come to the attention of the authorities, he has protested his innocence and never yet faced prison. If I get caught, I've failed. I pull the label from the waist of the jeans to check the price tag again. No way can I pay. Maybe I should put these costly clothes back on the rails to wait for someone who can afford them.

The door to the changing room is a grey painted shutter and peering through the slats I can see that no one else is up here, but then I hear heels and jangly bangles approaching. The voice of the glossy-lipped Debbie Harry lookalike purrs through the door, "How are you getting on?"

"Trying to make up my mind," I giggle as if she'd cracked a joke.

"Let me know if you need any help."

"Can you tell me how fast you can run?"

Of course, I don't say that, but it's what I'm thinking as I hear her heels tip tapping the floor as she walks away. I reckon her shiny black stilettos will slow her down a fair bit should she decide to leg it after me.

Try to figure out my options. I could stuff the clothes into my bag and attempt to walk casually out of the shop. But the plastic carrier's not big enough, the bulk of the jeans will protrude, no good. Picture myself handcuffed and pushed by coppers into the back of their van whilst disapproving shoppers look on. Try telling myself that it's not worth the risk but the thought of leaving the shop with my mission unaccomplished weighs me down. Lean my damp forehead on the cold mirror. Think, what would Dad do?

Dad has instilled a moral manifesto around crime: never steal from an individual or small business but big business and governments are fair game. *Take any chance you can to get one over on them.* This is opportunity knocks, I tell myself. No store detective and two assistants, not much older than me, who probably don't care if an item or two goes astray. And Chelsea Girl is not a girl, she's a big fat corporation run by men in suits with loads more money than me. I'm their charitable donation. A new plan hatches: keep the outfit on, put my old shit clothes on top, that way the Faircost carrier bag is as light and empty as when I walked in.

The shop music changes to Dexy's Midnight Runners, "C'mon Eileen" and I sing along, changing the lyrics to "C'mon Aisling". The music gods are calling me to action. It's happening. I pull my baggy, beige jumper over the top of the shirt and my deepening red face. Think of my parents' wrath if I get caught, but still I keep going, pulling my navy-blue crimplene trousers over the jeans, the beat of the music spurring me on. I look bulky wearing two layers, and nerves are off the scale as I swing through the shutters of the changing room door. Try to walk casually down the stairs to the ground floor, hoping the shop assistants won't notice that I've put on "weight". Sunlight is shining through the windows and the wide glass doorway signalling my exit is only a few feet away. Turn to look at Debbie Harry, who is now stood by the till with a hanger in her hand. Her eyes scan me as she smiles, an automatic glassy-eyed smile, "Any good?"

I mean to say, "Sorry, I left them upstairs, should I have brought them down? Would you be able to put them by for me and I'll pop back later?" Instead, I make a whimpering sound and pray that the beat of "C'mon Eileen" has drowned it out. I follow the whimper with a "no, sorry" and hear the fearful wobble in my voice. I've forgotten to breathe. Oh Christ, I think she's on to me, but she says nothing, just keeps smiling her strange, vacant smile. I walk past her and make it through the front doors with no alarm sounding.

The daylight is blinding after the low lights of the shop. I gulp in air and walk as fast as possible up the hill, past Boots and Marks & Sparks, towards the bus stop, expecting a hand to land on my shoulder at any moment.

Feel the heat from the layers of clothes turning my body sweaty and damp. Bet my pits pong but can't afford to drop the pace because I can see the number 17, my unsuspecting get-away vehicle, at the stop already filling up.

By the time I board the bus the adrenaline rush has subsided. I climb to the top-deck and sit in the front row seat, feeling proud and relieved as the bus pulls away and rumbles towards home. I got away with it! In my head I can hear the voices of the kids who always have nice clothes. They're asking me, *Where did you buy that shirt and those jeans?* I smile and say, *My dad bought them for me.*

Next day Mam asks where I got the new outfit hanging in my wardrobe. I decide to tell her the truth.

"I got them from Chelsea Girl."

"And where did you get the money?"

Telling her the full story is a touch risky because she's inclined to go through the motions of reacting like a normal parent, but I like to give her cause to worry. It's the only time she gives me her full attention.

The interrogation takes place in the kitchen. It's just me, Mam and Dad. The other kids have all left home. The rule in our house is that when you turn sixteen you must find your own digs, and I'm soon to reach the age of out-stayed welcome. Older brothers, Seamus and Thomas, born within two years of each other, and almost ten years ahead of me, are long gone. Older sister Caitlin, Mam's favourite, has recently fallen from grace, having left home to move in with her boyfriend. Mam and Dad say she is *living in sin,* although they don't really believe in all that hell and heaven stuff and never go to Mass. But they tell me to keep quiet about it in case news of her shame should make its way across the water to our relatives in Ireland.

Back to question time and too long a silence as Mam waits for my answer. I look at Dad, who is filling the kettle, and then back at Mam, who is wiping crumbs from the kitchen table with intense concentration. I scratch at the label on the bottle of HP Sauce and make a little tear.

"I took them." She stops wiping. "I stole them."

"You stole them?"

She looks at Dad with her cross face on: dark eyebrows furrowed, jaw muscles tight, cheeks turning pink. He plonks the kettle down on the gas ring, strikes a match, then looks at me with his hugely amused face on: eyes glinting with mischief, mouth in a half smile. "How did you do that?"

I describe how I checked out the joint to see if I was being watched, how I had considered my options, and then seized my chance. His approving laugh is as warm as the lit gas.

"Jesus! What if you'd got caught?" Mam's voice is rising to shrill. Unlike Dad, Mam yearns for respectability, security and a law-abiding life. One in which the gas does not suddenly get cut off because the authorities discover that someone has illegally re-routed the supply. Knowing that any day the police, Inland Revenue or Social Security might come knocking keeps her in a state of constant stress. Her biggest worry is saying the 'wrong thing' and dropping Dad in it. I sometimes worry about that too, but mostly I like being the one who answers the phone and pretends he isn't home. He loves it when I do that. It makes him laugh.

He's laughing now and I can see his reaction casting doubt in Mam's mind on how she should respond. She settles for a pointing finger and a "Don't you ever do that again. You'll end up in jail."

Dad adds, with a wink, "And if you do, you're on your own, we'll not be visiting."

Later that evening we sit in front of the television, digesting the roast and chuckling our way through an episode of *Only Fools and Horses*. As the credits roll and the News begins, Mam nips out to the kitchen to make a cup of tea. Dad is settled in his favourite leather-look armchair, a glass of Bell's whiskey on the go. He leans forward as an item on election results in Ulster is reported. Gerry Adams appears and a crowd cheers.

"You know, I always thought you took after your mother, but I think you're more like me, a rebel."

Me, the last in line, crowned rebel. The word conjures up Robin Hood; it joins with songs of the Irish rebellion that Dad likes to sing. His blue eyes, warmed by the whisky, smile at me, "You did well today."

"But what if I'd been caught?"

"Sure, there's always that fear but if you box clever, and listen to your dad, you'll not get caught, and if you do, just deny it. Remember, *there is nothing either good or bad, but thinking makes it so*."

Dad's habit of quoting Shakespeare really gets going after a whisky. Sometimes he's Hamlet, other times Mark Antony, but most often he's Macbeth. And he loves a monologue.

"Would you listen to your man there, slagging off Adams. What does he know? Typical ignorance of the English establishment. The whole system is crooked Aisling. You have to learn how to beat it. But don't worry, your dad will show you how."

"The Changing Room" is an extract from Bridget Keehan's novel Identity Theft.

Fifty miles an hour

Alix Edwards

"Your hair's disgusting. You could fry an egg on it,"
Rebecca Jones giggles. Her friends clap like performing
seals. I inch away from them into the corridor, past men
in suits whose eyes stay glued to their Financial Times and
women in well-cut office outfits and court shoes. I feel
stupid in my too-small uniform. I hate my school and I
hate this train.

We pull into Ascot station. I push the window down,
turn the cold silver handle to open the door and tread
from the metal step: straight into a puddle. Cold water
seeps through the crack in the sole of my left shoe. Ice-
cold drizzle grazes my face.

Cars pull up outside the station. Doors swing open.
Parents wave. I watch the other kids climb onto dry back
seats. They are lucky. I brace myself for the windswept
walk uphill.

It's rush hour. My side of the road is packed bumper to bumper. It stinks of petrol and rotting leaves. The other side is dark and empty. I walk faster than the cars that crawl beside me. I want to get out of the cold. Patches of heat leave their bonnets. Their engines growl. I recognise some of the kids from my class. They wave, but no-one offers me a lift.

The damp winter air creeps under my shirt-cuffs, up my sleeves and sears my skin. I turn my collar up. The wind blows my too-short skirt. A white van honks. A middle-aged man rolls his window down and whistles, "Want a lift, luv?" I run past red taillights that snake up the hill. I look through giant silhouettes of naked trees. A blue car with a taxi sign speeds down the hill towards me. It stops in the middle of the street and beeps. It does a U-turn and keeps honking until another car lets it in. Ma leaps out. Her obsidian eyes look weird. "Hurry up, Maria. Get in!"

They let us through a reinforced glass door. "This is no place for children," the nurse pushes me aside. A glucose drip feeds my dad. Her eyes narrow as she adjusts the intravenous pole but Dad says nothing in our defence because he is dead or near enough. His body lies buried in stiff cellular blankets. There's a small TV screen next to him on wheels. He sprouts a spaghetti junction tangle of white wires and plastic tubes. The green monitor lines zigzag downwards every few beats instead of climbing up.

His grey face is impassive. His glassy eyes stare up to heaven. The nurse scribbles in his notes and shakes her head, "Poor thing." There are charts on a clipboard at the end of his bed.

Dad's awake! Every afternoon I trudge up that hill,
turn left at the top and continue past the shops and the
racecourse, through grey polished corridors until I reach
Ward D. The hospital is warm. It smells of stale food and
disinfectant. The back of the ward has French doors, and
rabbits play on the lawn outside.

They wheel in the heavy silver trolley, The orderly
hands me a plastic tray. I remove the metal cover from
the scalding hot plate. Beef with mashed potatoes and
cabbage. Orange jelly for pudding. Dad can't eat that, he's
diabetic. "You have it!" he says. "Don't tell Mum." I chop
up his meat and spoon feed him like a baby. I wipe his
chin with a stiff white napkin where the gravy dribbles out
and read him *The Spy Who Came in from the Cold* from one of
his large print books.

Sometimes I see the next train go past when I walk up
the High Street. I pass the crossing where the car hit him.
I wonder how it feels to fly through the air for fifty feet
but no-one ever talks about how it happened.

Weeks have passed and Dad's still in hospital. "Why
don't you get a removal company to pack your stuff for
you?" Elsie from next door stares at us with disdain. She
knows we can't afford it and anyway there's no point as
we have to sell nearly everything to pay the bills and Ma's
furniture won't fit in our tiny new house. We put a card in
the newsagent's then get boxes from Bejam and stick them
shut with brown tape.

"Do you like my new curtains?" Elsie waves. Ma locks

the front door. "*Stronza!* Bitch!" She raises her hand in the sign of the horns, then sinks into Dad's armchair, wails and moans and stamps her feet. "I will not lose this house," she screams but it was lost months ago along with Dad's job, the day the doctor said Dad would never walk again.

We wheel Dad up a scaffold-board ramp through the frosted glass front door into a narrow hallway. The metal footplates from his wheelchair scrape the wallpaper.

Ma puts the kettle on. We start unpacking boxes. Half our furniture is gone and the tiny square living room is still stuffed fuller than a museum. "*Madonna benedetta!* You cannot swing a cat in here!"

Dad does not speak to anyone anymore. He chain-smokes all day and sits in the kitchen hunched over his talking books machine listening to spy stories. When I get back from school, I have to empty the Murano glass ashtray, stuffed full with cigarette butts, into the kitchen bin and make him a cup of tea with pellets and Carnation condensed milk.

Ma comes home late every night, so I have to cook dinner: Bejam special offer frozen sausages with runner beans, frozen carrots with steak and kidney pie, no pudding, two slices of bread or boiled potatoes which I weigh on his special scales, because they are carbohydrates. He moves from the kitchen to the living room to watch TV, even though he can no longer see it, and I bring him his food on a tray. When Ma gets back, she eats the leftovers, falls asleep on the sofa and snores.

I have to get up early too, to do a paper round which I hate when it's cold, but still there's not enough money to go out like we used to or eat anything nice, let alone buy fashionable clothes like everyone else at school.

The district nurse snaps her black bag shut. She's made Dad join a blind people's pottery class. "He needs to get out more," she insists. Dad's wheeled into a minibus every Monday afternoon and brings home crooked pots decorated with nails. "What is this *strafanici*?" Ma looks at them in disgust and puts them in the shed.

The garden is long and thin. An orchard stretches out along the back to an embankment with the railway line. I hear trains rumble past. Their windows are lit up at night.

"You're lucky your father is still alive," croon the social worker and volunteer from Red Cross, our only other visitors, apart from the talking books man, now we live on the wrong side of town. "Does luck mean not being invited to parties anymore and looking like a jumble sale?" I yell. Dad looks up. I think I see him smile. "I don't know what is wrong with that child!" Ma sniffs. Now I know why Dad calls them idiots.

"You have to adapt," the District Nurse gives me that concerned look. Some things are OK, like not having to run up that hill in the pouring rain to get the train in the morning, not having to see Rebecca Jones or the rest of those bitches, getting up ten minutes later, now I can walk to school, but Bracknell is ugly, this house is cold and the kitchen table is too small to fit the talking book machine and my homework.

I miss the song of the Grandstand clock and the excitement of Race Days. I miss hiding behind the curtains and laughing as the punters walk past in top hats and flouncy dresses. I miss the fields, the smell of autumn and the giant trees. But most of all, I miss not being normal any more.

Into the Blackwood: character sketches from the Valleys

Simone Greenwood

MANDY

Keeps a lipstick in the pocket of her tabard –

Comes in handy, see, in case a man in uniform pops in
Go and ask if he's single, is it? Go on, ask him...
but don't tell him I sent you, mind, just act casual

Keeps her tea mug hidden in an empty bucket –

Comes in handy, see, in case the boss walks in unexpected
 – Aren't you allowed a cuppa? Bet she's having one!
She's a miserable cow, she is, anything to catch us out

Keeps the place spotless, stair nosing Brasso-bright –

Looks impressive, see, when the punters arrive after work
 – Not gonna lie, this place would be buzzing without you
Too bloody right! But do they appreciate me? Like hell they do

MIKE

Small world! That's where I grew up
haven't been back for years
got a cousin still lives there though
Still rough?
  — *Round the edges, yeah*
What made you want to live there?
  — *Take it you don't approve of my life choices then?*
Didn't mean it like that, it's just
I was driven, you know ... to get out
seems weird someone wants to —
  — *Get in?*
Look, I grew up cold and hungry
never want to feel that again
so I work
don't stop, even though the missus says I should
We're moving to Dubai soon
  — *Dubai? God, I'd hate to live there*

MR JONES

No matter how your day was going
he had the kind of smile that made you
feel happy and smile back

A sunny smile and a wave, out by his car
a 1989 petrol blue Fiesta
one suit-wearing owner since new
oil changed like clockwork

We exchanged no words
no particulars were known
just each other's smiles and the sense
that his bones ached, and that is all

I liked the familiarity of seeing him
on my way out or way home

before the pandemic hit

Now I look at his house on Rightmove
feels like an intrusion of sorts
see his teak furniture and knick-knacks
the pattern of his carpet, his curtains
the stairs he climbed at night

All these particulars known but
I'd rather his smile

CERI

Pink-slippered feet on the pavement
dogs barking behind the fence

I'LL BE THERE NOW IN A MINUTE

Want feeding they do, hungry buggers
Between them and the kids I'll be eaten
out of house and home
Have you seen the prices down ASDA's?
Three pound fifty for ketchup ... for ketchup!
Bloody cheek calling that a rollback
They can roll back up my arse, I'm telling you!

Winter Wynn Gardens

Ben Huxley

Constant cold air flows as if from a broken tap that
fluctuates between jets and drips. On the grey concrete
path is a light brown blotch. Two hours ago, a lad in
school uniform gulped an unmeasured mix of voddy
and lemonade into a stomach of Coco-Pops and advent
calendar chocolate, then retched it onto the path as his
group cheered and clapped before noting how it steamed
like piss. He was embarrassed, and he silently vowed to get
better at drinking. He will. Now the same group is playing
Rugby in Ysgol Bryn Elian's field, tipsy but they're getting
away with it, and the sick has ceased to steam, leaving a
dry, cold brown patch that every dog this morning has
stopped at. On the other side of the public garden is
a smashed pumpkin, so flat it looks two-dimensional,
painted on the ground, half rotted but the recent cold
snap preserves it. The trees tower above the scene. Some

branches are bare and black, with a few brown leaves clinging to the extremities. The evergreen trees and bushes look like they want to laugh at their neighbours' nakedness, but they're too cold for such frivolity. Instead they bristle along with the grass, still dusted by the dead leaves of the autumn, dry and flirting with frostiness, just like everything else in early winter Wynn Gardens.

***

A girl who should be in college sits on a bench, scrolling the endless scroll. The wind licks her fingers and conjures memories of washing her hands in her grandparents' kitchen where there wasn't hot water. She would dread the pressure on her bladder, knowing it would lead to numbing and stiffening her hands as she tried to make soapy lather in cold water. She would hold it in for as long as possible, enduring both the need to wee and the repeats of *Bullseye*, sitting on that couch... that couch with the tassels of string she used to wrap around her finger... A sharp gust brings her back to the present, to the gardens, to her phone. She's been scrolling without reading for a few minutes so she refreshes the homepage to see what she's missed. The tweet at the top of her feed reads *I believe this is acceptable now, right?* followed by a heavily filtered photograph of a gingerbread latte from Starbucks. 10k likes, 2k comments, 931 retweets. She doesn't like the sentiment but taps the heart to like it, just in case karma exists. After tapping her profile to see if she's missed anything, she stares at her tweet from an hour ago: *I'm having a difficult day today. If anyone could send positive vibes then that would be much appreciated.* She was sure it got a like five minutes ago, but it's either been deleted or she imagined it, and she doesn't know which is worse. It's a dead tweet, unlikely to get anything. She deletes it. Her "pinned tweet" reads *Hey, I'm Laura — an aspiring journalist based in the beautiful North Wales coast. Follow me for local news, local scenery, and (of course) cats.* She wonders if it's too desperate. She didn't want a Twitter account because none of her friends were on it, but her college tutor made the whole class set one up for career prospects. Now she can't get off it. She taps open Facebook Messenger for the first time in a couple of weeks and finds the unread message from a girl she hopes is still her best friend. She taps at the keyboard: *Hey, I'm so sorry for not replying to your last message. Sounds like you had a mad one. Good night, yeh? I hate to do this but are you free? I'm having a tough day and don't know where else to go. I promise I'll be a better friend xxxx* her thumb hovers above the send button, then over the delete, back and forth, back, and forth.

***

A gust rustles the leaves but doesn't lift them much. It barely moves the grass. It certainly doesn't move the ornamental elms or the evergreen shrubs. The breeze does, however, blow a plastic wrapper into the gardens, where the only other foreign objects are puke and pumpkin. It dances a spiral dance, twirling. Ironically, it was once home to a Curly Wurly. It glides across the grass to the other side of the gardens, where it flips back and goes to another corner. Like a dog, it circles a tree before gliding towards another bench, where it catches the eye of a lad in low rise jeans, a hoodie, and a beanie hat, sharing a joint with his friend in a tracksuit who sits on a wooden bench, a round tree trunk missing a right-angle chunk.

"Fock *me*, didn't know they still made 'em," he says.

"Eh?" his friend says.

"Curly Wurlies," Beanie Hat nods towards the wrapper, "thought they was a thing of the past like, but there's a wrapper down there, all new lookin' in the leaves. Not an old wrapper, that. They must still make 'em."

"Oi, stop changin' the subject whenever I start winnin' the argument, you always do that, just so *you* can think yuv won," says Tracksuit.

Beanie Hat sighs and watches the wrapper dance away, out of the garden, content that it finally got some attention. He passes the joint, and says:

"So am not happy that the homeless people are cold, right, am not happy 'bout that."

"Yeh are tho!" snaps Tracksuit, and drags the joint a bit too hard. "Yeh just said, ah can quote yer lad, yeh said like ten seconds ago – *am actually* happy *that homeless people have to wrap up a bit warmer* – yeh just said it!"

"Right, okay, yeh that was some bad wordin' I'll admit that. But what ah meant by it was the climate, it's good that it's finally gettin' cold in the winter in Wales like it should be. Shows the planet's not completely focked."

"But why's it a bad fing to just get a bit warmer for the people livin' on the streets, why can't you admit that maybe they were enjoyin' it for a bit, thankful it's warm in the winter. And now it's cold as fock again, and there's you all like *thank fock* – livin' in yer warm house, only leavin' to pick up weed or buy a Twix or a Monster."

"But you got to admit it's better overall, lad." Beanie Hat accepts the joint, the passing of which is a ritual that transcends the most heated of disagreements. "If global warmin' carries on, there won't be any streets left, they'll all be flooded, the planet's dyin' man, an' it'll be them on the street that suffer worst when it dies, yeh? So it *is* a good thing that it's cold cuz the planet isn't dyin' *just* yet."

"Just listen to yurself man. Mah dad was on the streets in the eighties, back when he lived in Milton Keynes," Tracksuit accepts the joint but doesn't break his flow, "he used to tell me that the nights were so fockin' cold an' he just wanted to curl up in his sleepin' bag, but he couldn't cuz that was his dinner time, when the clubs an' bars closed an' the rich cunts bought chips from the chippy an' threw half 'em away, that was his chance to go though the bins an' get food, an' it was so cold an' he just wanted to wrap up an' lie down, but it was his *only* chance to..."

But Beanie Hat isn't listening, because his mind is half an hour in the future, where he's sitting in his gaming chair, freshly baked, booting up *Rainbow Six: Vegas* on his 360 with a can of Monster at his side and six Curly Wurlies on his desk.

***

The constant breeze is so slight that she sounds like a wheeze, a gas leak, oozing through the leaves and branches and evergreen shrubs and grass. She nudges the plants, who bounce back with defiance. It'll take more than a little breeze to uproot them. A small human left off her reins on a kicking frenzy, maybe, or a puppy off his lead. But not a light winter breeze like her, who drifts gently like a lost soul through the garden, along the paths, through the grass, under the trees, swirling up the trunk then dropping down into the Midsummer Beauty and Great Orme shrubbery, between the tiny leaves and twigs and insects. She feels it all as her essence surrounds it, the tiny lives, the micro-city of sap and green and muck and creature, all alive. She leaves the bush and finds herself back on the path, gliding forward, under the curvy concrete pergola towards a figure on a bench, a woman wrapped in four layers, who feels her chill and shivers but doesn't mind. In fact, she is comforted by her embrace.

This woman is a mum of three who has escaped the pandemonium of home to sit in Wynn Gardens, as she does every day at this time in the mid-afternoon. Thankful of her gloves and scarf, she clutches her knees and takes a deep breath, as the voice in her headphones has told her to. She practices mindfulness not for herself, but for her partner who sometimes cries, and her kids, who she hopes won't need counselling someday. She's trying to fix herself for them. She downloaded this app for them. The voice in her ears blends with the voice in her head which merges with ephemeral sensations inside and out...

...and just notice the sensations of your breath in your nose as you breathe in, and out got to be my mouth broke my nose in a fight with Sophie Morris in year eight septum fucked up need to get it fixed operated on but turn down the addictive painkillers this time and just have the paracetamol or ibuprofen because you'll get addicted

again and you've been doing well, no junk for two years
and no coke for eight months keep going keep going
self-improvement soon you'll be the best mum and best
girlfriend you're better sober some people can drink
some can't you can't, God I could do with a drink I can
smell the pub from here, stale carpets, ale, hate ale but it
smells of the pub where they sell gin and rum and voddy
and I could call Cath tonight she'd get a drink with me
she doesn't know I'm quitting I'll tell Dan and the kids
I'm staying at Kim's or Jackie's and get rat-arsed in the
deep breaths now, in and out Jesus control yourself control
your impulses just feel the breathing in your throat a bit
scratchy itchy cough don't cough cold the start of a cold
can't give it to the kids it's almost Christmas we don't
want to be ill can't visit Dan's parents if we're ill he'll cry
he hasn't seen them for months he's been working living
his dream career the lucky *now, it's understandable if you get lost
in thought* fuck's sake focus focus focus *don't punish yourself,
just observe the thought* it's okay, it's all okay you're in Wynn
Gardens you're in your happy place, you're safe *now I want
you to open your eyes and observe your surroundings* here I am, I'm
here *wherever you are, observe the colours and shapes* the Kidney
Vetch and Bird's Foot Trefoil, the Kidney has a Latin
name I've forgotten but it translates to Wound Healer and
I wish it would...

　...This goes on for a while longer, and she soon gets
a focus on the present moment and relaxes. The session
on the app comes to an end, but she remains seated there
on the bench listening to the breeze and the distant birds
and sea. Staring at the darkness behind her eyes she
remembers a scene from her childhood. The first time

she ever slept over at a friend's house, they couldn't sleep so they talked in the pitch black, a deep darkness in the deep countryside that she'd never experienced before. They looked at the darkness together and noticed how shapes made of faint light disappear when you stare at them for too long. They half fell asleep and half dreamed together, talking nonsense that sounded like wisdom, or the other way around, before one of them, then both of them, drifted off.

She opens her eyes and it's darker than when she closed them, a lot darker, and the orange glow of the streetlamp lights up a patch on the grass. It reminds her of a shape from some point in her memory that she can't place. Childhood maybe. It's safe.

***

The sun has sunk and the same boys from the morning turn up to finish the voddy and lemonade. It's dark in the gardens now, and they light up their patch with the torches on their phones. The brown patch catches the eye of one of them, who cheers at the memory of ten hours prior, the chunder before school that preceded a half-drunk PE lesson. It was only this morning, they say, but it seems like years ago, a lifetime ago. Cars drive past on Abergele Road, roaring, beeping, and one of the boys plays music on his phone. They're cold but they're excited to drink, one of them more keen than the others to prove his mettle. He rubs his hands but he'll never be warm in there, not with the constant flow of the icy chill through winter Wynn Gardens.

New Year's Eve at The Nun's Purse

Amy Kitcher

If there's a dingier, grottier pub in all the British Isles, I've not found it yet. The Nun's Purse boasts fly-strewn windowsills, walls the colour of a tobacco addict's teeth, and table tops so sticky that old Bill Jones lost a shirt sleeve to one this afternoon. Even the most iron guts can't stomach "The Food", not for long anyway, and never twice. The toilets? Don't ask.

Complaining is futile. The Manager — Tommy "Gun" Benson — has industrial deafness.

Should deafness not be obstacle enough, try bitching about lipstick smeared wine glasses to a retired artilleryman who survived on starvation rations as a Korean prisoner in a war camp and see if your "customer experience" improves.

A thick layer of soggy grey sawdust carpets the pub's flagstones. Tommy claims lumbago prevents him mopping up slops. Maybe it does. Maybe it doesn't. I'm sure as hell not going to argue with him. But month-old sawdust has limits, and seepage from a dozen bags of bloody meat will breach them, no problemo. The macabre bags are coveted prizes for the bingo, held annually in aid of a bowel cancer charity.

I don't play meat bingo. Winning five pounds of raw animal flesh is way down my list of priorities, somewhere below "Attend Ladies Day at Ascot" but above "Shave a Hungry Rottweiler". It took seven years of explaining "veg-an-ism" to Treasure (so called because of her sunken chest) before she stopped waving bingo cards under my nose. The woman wouldn't take a hint if it was a winning lottery ticket.

Despite my anti-meat stance, I'm as much a fixture of the New Year tableau as the leaking crimson bags. Each year, I leave civilisation and undertake the pilgrimage home. I consider it my own Camino de Santiago de Compostela, but with less sun, fewer scallop shells and no hair shirts. My bar stool is reserved and I always drink a White Russian. The ritual is as enduring as my fight with frizzy hair. Both are legacies from my mother.

The hair is genetic. The White Russian — and the shuddersome meat bags — are legal testaments to my mother's dark sense of humour. I own the pub on the condition I return on New Year's Eve and raise a toast with the sickly-sweet cocktail. What's more, the feat must be witnessed — to the amusement of the peg-toothed natives — by Mr Atkinson, the solicitor.

If I don't submit to my mother's will, possession of *The Nun's Purse* reverts to the landowner, Lord Bainbridge, who's made no secret about wanting to flatten it and build luxury accommodation for his "gentleman's shooting retreats". And I'm not talking the clay pigeon variety here, people. As a vegan, I'm stuck. I can't have the blood of all those game birds on my hands, so I sacrifice my New Year's Eve on the altar of my clear conscience.

There I was. Leant against the bar, eyeballing the door ready to make free and easy with the scowls when in rushes Lewis Hardcastle. He's not the solicitor, but my A-class grimace doesn't go to waste either. Every year, Lewis — my teenage crush — necks a pint of Guinness, ignores me, and leaves. His presence is as regular as any bag of tenderloin, but at least the sight of him doesn't make me want to vomit.

The icy wind grabs the door and slams it behind him. People jump. Beer flies. More spillages for the overtaxed sawdust. When Lewis has everyone's attention, he puffs out his chest, staples a thousand-yard stare to his face, and bulldozes his way to the bar searching for trouble.

Yes, Lewis' gunslinger entry was way over the top. Yes, the jukebox stuttered and a tumbleweed rolled out from behind the bar. But don't get distracted by the melodrama.

That was my first mistake.

Lewis approaches like a heat-seeking missile with its sights locked on target. I glance down. The novelty Christmas jumper with flashing lights and silver baubles on my breasts doesn't seem so funny now. Seriously, I look like a landing strip. I only wore the hideous thing because Mr Atkinson always turns up in Armani and I wanted to make it clear I consider the legal formalities to be a farce.

I fiddle with the hem of my jumper, scanning the pub for a friendly face, someone, anyone, to sidle over to and engage in conversation. Only Toby — an overweight guide dog whose master has worn a rut in the road between his house and the pub — meets my eye. Even bloody-bingo Treasure has stopped shooting me daggers. *Typical.*

Lewis skids to a halt, boot-clad feet spread wide. He's got the build of a tighthead prop, all muscled shoulders and broad chest. He played rugby for the county and I'd go along in all weathers and cheer. *Because I was a pathetic loser.*

"You gotta come, Selma. I need you."

I consider ignoring him but — Christmas jumper aside — I'm not *that* childish.

"Why?" My voice squeaks like a hinge needing oil, in contrast to his, which is as rich and earthy as a peat whisky poured over crushed ice.

"Petra's whelping and the pups are breech. The vet's snowed in. I can't afford to lose this litter."

"I need to wait for the solicitor."

"That wank stain's not gunna be here for hours. The Pass is closed. Please, Selma. I need you."

"Not brought my kit."

"I need your eyes, dammit! Your hands." Lewis holds up his own in frustration. I've seen smaller shovels. He steps towards me, close enough for the clean, sharp scent of his aftershave to slice through the foetid stink of the pub like Death's scythe. The crease between his eyes deepens to a furrow. "I thought you cared about saving animals."

"I do! But gun dogs... You know my views on shooting!

Half of Bainbridge's business comes from people wanting to hunt with 'Hardcastle's Famous Vizslas.'" I do the air-quote thing and Lewis' lip curls in disgust.

"So you'll let Petra die to score one over Bainbridge?" A mixture of anger, pain and sadness move across Lewis' rugged face faster than a cold weather front.

I sigh dramatically. Glance at the clock. 9.34 p.m. Look at Tommy slowly smearing glasses with a stained tea towel. Take in the booze-wizened regulars who choose the world's shittiest drinking hole over their own homes.

I down my drink and slam the glass on the bar.

The barn is a mile from the pub, but a further forty-three light years in comparative cosiness. Warm and dark, it smells of straw and earth. Horses whicker, stamping and shifting in their stalls. I follow the bobbing circle of light from Lewis' torch and remember standing behind him in the dinner queue (after fighting Tracy Tanner for the prestigious spot) checking out his bum and fantasising about running my fingers through the thick black curls at his nape.

"She's through here."

He flicks the light into a stall, but I already hear the dog growling. Petra's a beauty. Pale bronze coat, long legs, and ears the size of handkerchiefs.

I kneel before the whelping crate and her growling kicks up a gear. Lewis holds her head as I run my hands over her trembling, velveteen body. Such a placid girl, she doesn't try to nip me and stoically accepts my examination

"She's exhausted," I whisper.

"Been over eight hours."

"I'll need more light."

Lewis stands up and leaves. I rock back on my heels and shuck off my coat. The red and green fairy lights reflect in the dog's solemn brown eyes. I should take the damn jumper off, too, but my vest is embarrassingly tatty.

A fluorescent strip buzzes overhead and flickers to life, bathing the narrow stall in a yellow glow. Petra keeps up her deep rumbling growl. Her glossy fur twitches like she's being bitten by invisible ants.

"Anything else?" Lewis asks from the doorway.

"Oil. For my hands."

He returns clutching two bottles. One is baby oil, the other is olive. He offers both and I choose the olive. Normally I would question why a single man needs baby oil, but I'll make an exception for Lewis. The temperature in the stall rises a few degrees. The heat source? My face.

I roll up my sleeves. I'm halfway through oiling my hands and wrists when he nods at my jumper.

"Do those lights turn off? They might frighten Petra."

I peer down at my breasts, which are — yep — gaudier than the Blackpool illuminations. "Not sure. They're movement activated." I jiggle my shoulders side to side and the flashing increases. "See?"

His dark eyes scope-lock on my chest and his Adam's apple bobs like a buoy on a windy lake. "Is there a battery?" he asks quietly, running a hand through his hair.

"Not sure. Electronics aren't my thing."

"Can I try?"

I nod and hold still while Lewis lifts my jumper and slides his big, warm hands inside. As he fumbles around searching for the battery pack, my fourteen-year-old self spins cartwheels in delight. His eyes crinkle in concentration and the hint of a smile curls the corner of his mouth.

"Any luck?"

"No, the battery's sewn into the seam."

"I'll take it off." Mindless of my oily hands, I yank the jumper over my head, ball it up and hide it underneath my coat. Too late, I recall my tatty vest also has a lovely Hello Kitty pattern... Lewis, to his credit, gives the cartoon cat no more than a confused squint before we hunker down to business.

He cradles Petra's head and I slide an oiled hand into her birth canal. The amniotic sac's burst, so all I need to do is wait for the lull between contractions to hook my fingers beneath the pup's rear legs and manoeuvre them into position. Once the first pup is born, Petra's able to deliver the others unaided. Lewis and I sit side by side, fizzing with our shared victory, and watch as she licks the squirming bundles clean and they nose their way to her teats.

"Thanks."

"No problem. Got to get back to the pub, though. Where's the best place to wash?"

"In the house. Come on." He grabs my jumper and coat.

The kitchen is clean and tidy. A huge oak table takes up most of the space, flanked by a bench on one side and a row of mismatched chairs on the other. The place is pretty. Pastel colours, floral curtains, and a hint of gingham. No wonder Lewis can only tolerate the foulness of The Nun's Purse for a single pint.

I scrub the blood from my hands and dry them on a pink towel, toasty from the Aga. Lewis' presence at my back makes my neck tingle and my clothes feel too tight.

When I turn he's holding a bottle of whisky in his hands. Single malt. Good stuff.

"For helping," he says, pushing the bottle towards me.

"I don't want it."

"I have to give you something. To say thanks."

"No need," I say, putting on my coat and zipping it up.

Halfway to the door, he seizes my shoulder and pulls me back. "Wait!"

He brings his face close to mine and points at the ceiling. I glance up. A sprig of mistletoe hangs above our heads. *Uchelwydd* the old people call it, believing it keeps evil spirits at bay. The old farmhouse creaks around us. A clock ticks in the next room.

Slowly, achingly slowly, Lewis Hardcastle lowers his lips to mine.

His kiss is soft. His hands are gentle as they stroke my neck, rising to sift through my hair, making my scalp tingle. A decade of yearning distilled into a moment's pleasure. His arms, muscled from years of throwing hay bales around, are granite under my hands. The feel of them tethers me to the ground.

"I wanted to kiss you since the day you climbed on the roof of the history Portakabin to rescue that lame pigeon," he murmurs, his breath hot against my neck.

Take that Tracy Tanner! "Why didn't you?"

"I couldn't. I was in a bad place and you were… perfect. I needed to believe in something perfect. It helped me through." He thumbs my cheek and presses his forehead to mine. "You helped me through, Selma."

"Through what?"

He tenses and pulls away. The furrow between his brow deepens. "A dark time."

I sense there's more, but I don't push. "What kind of place are you in now?"

He lets out a long breath. "A good one," he says, rocking his hips against me. "The best, perhaps..." He raises an eyebrow, a question all in itself.

We hold hands as we follow the bobbing torch light through the twisting lanes back to the pub. The world is sparkling for us, from the star-spangled sky to the diamond-glint of frost in the air. Snow crusts my boots and every step is heavier than the last. The shining windows of The Nun's Purse are fuzzy orange squares against the darkness and I experience a heady rush of affection for the grotty old pub. I'll spend more time here, help Tommy do the place up. Pay a cleaner from the village.

A Range Rover is parked on the verge. Someone has scrawled "wanker" in the thin snow on the rear window. My heart dips.

We push through the door to find the place silent. Empty, except for Tommy and Mr Atkinson the solicitor, whose beautiful three-piece Armani fails to distract from the fact he's got a face like a bag of smashed crabs.

"Evening, Selma."

Lewis tenses, standing tall and still as an English Pointer scenting a game bird. I whirl around. Bainbridge

— the sly, fat fucker — is perched on a stool next to the door. His bespoke tweed and handmade shiny brogues are as inappropriate as a shotgun in a primary school.

I shudder. "Get out!"

"A poor greeting for someone who wants to make you rich." Bainbridge speaks as if he's addressing people across three counties and his gestures are so expansive he could marshal an aircraft. For Bainbridge, subtlety is a disease affecting other people.

"I've told you. I'm not interested in selling."

"Selma —" says Tommy, but Bainbridge cuts him off.

"Think of the jobs it'll bring! The inward investment!" He flings an arm. "Surely you understand people here need this, Selma?"

"Not. Interested. In. Selling." Some folk can't understand normal accents, so it pays to repeat oneself s-l-o-w-l-y and LOUDLY.

"But this place —" Bainbridge swivels his head in a manner not unlike the little girl possessed by the Devil in *The Exorcist*. I'm *not* exaggerating. "— is disgusting." He's not exaggerating.

Tommy coughs meaningfully, picks up a handful of empties, and retreats behind the bar.

Yes, The Nun's Purse is battered and shabby, but so are the customers. So is Tommy. And perhaps — on the inside — so am I. We *need* this place, something Bainbridge will never understand.

"Last chance," he says, smoothing his tie. "Either accept the money —"

"Selma!" Lewis hisses, elbowing me. "The time!"

11.59pm. *Damn.*

"Quick, lass!" calls Tommy.

The White Russian is already on the bar. Tommy had it waiting all along. I swear I will never bemoan the man's dirt-blindness ever again. I dodge around the maze of tables and chairs and grab the stem of the cocktail glass. The drink is halfway to my lips when a firework bangs in the distance, followed by the pop and crackle of more happy pyrotechnics heralding the new year.

"Ah, Selma," says Bainbridge. "Midnight."

Mr Atkinson pipes up. "I'm sorry to inform you, Selma, as per the instructions in the last will and testament of Mrs ..." His monotonous recitation fades to a drone.

The room sways. My mother's complex web of legal intrigue has finally tripped me up. Bainbridge has won. I slump on a stool and rub my eyes.

Tommy rests a gnarled hand on my shoulder. "It's okay, lass," he murmurs. "Worse things in life."

A scream cuts through the shroud of my misery like a dressmaker's shears. Bainbridge is holding his face, blood pouring through his fingers and dripping down his tie. Lewis is shaking out his hand.

"You punched him?" I ask, distrusting my tear-filled eyes.

"I'll thue you!" Bainbridge hisses, pointing a trembling finger at Lewis. "You're all witnetheth!"

"Yeah? Try it. I'll go public. Take Selma's pub away? I'll go public. Understand?" Lewis shouts, the tendons in his neck straining. There's no deference in the way he sizes up Bainbridge, only raw, naked disgust.

Bainbridge narrows his streaming, piggy eyes and peers

at Lewis. "I have no idea what you're referring to."

"Yes, you do," Lewis replies. The icicles outside could learn a thing or two about frost from his voice.

"No, I —"

"Don't deny it! I *filmed* you," Lewis jabs a finger in the middle of Bainbridge's chest. "Rigged a camera in the hide, and another in the stable block."

"No!" Bainbridge stumbles backwards, knocks over a chair, and leaves a smear of blood on the wall. Not that it's noticeable against the general grime. You have to look *really* hard.

Lewis steps forward, again, and again until Bainbridge huddles in the corner. I always thought the fat toff imposing, but he shrinks when Lewis towers over him. "Do you want the world to know what a dirty —"

"I'll raise the rents! Everyone's rent! And evict you! I'll evict your whole family! They'll all suffer. Is that what you want, Hardcastle? Is it?"

"Your threats don't work on me anymore. Give up your claim to the pub or I'll tell the world what a perverted fucker you really are."

The silence stretches out, thin as gossamer, taut as razor wire. Tommy and Mr Atkinson stare open-mouthed at Lewis and Bainbridge, who are locked in a glaring contest. By the sounds of it, I'm the only one breathing, which is fine. I'm doing it hard and loud enough for the five of us.

"The other lads'll come forward. If I ask," says Lewis.

"Fine. I concede," Bainbridge replies in an uncharacteristically small voice. He hooks a finger in the knot of his tie and works it loose, before dabbing his nose with his handkerchief.

"Draft it, then," Lewis barks to Mr Atkinson. "I want it watertight. Tommy will witness."

"I don't have —"

"Now!"

The legal agreement between Lewis Hardcastle and Lord Aubin Fenston Bainbridge KStJ JP DL OBE RAC HMV GIF NASA is written on the back of a roll of Christmas wrapping paper. Bainbridge relinquishes all rights to The Nun's Purse and in exchange, Lewis will never make a *public* statement of any kind about his Lordship. Best of all? The new agreement means the pub's all mine. No caveats. No strings. No more New Year's Eve White Russian with witnesses.

"I want the recordings," Bainbridge says as he's leaving.

Lewis laughs. "Why? So you can get off to it again? Nah, I don't think so."

The door slams behind Bainbridge and Atkinson and the Range Rover roars away.

"You did sterling, lad," Tommy says, whipping the filthy tea towel off his shoulder and flinging it in the sink. "But don't leave it so late next time? Eh?"

"Shall we celebrate?" I ask them, hardly believing the shadow of Bainbridge has finally been exorcised.

"You two go ahead." Tommy's rheumy eyes flicker between us with a knowing glint. "But Himself gifted me an empty pub and I'll not waste the early night. I've a new Barbara Cartland, with pirates."

He heads upstairs, whistling a jaunty show tune.

I face my teenage crush surrounded by empty glasses and bloody sawdust. "Did Bainbridge hurt you?" I

whisper, eager and scared to fill in the blanks of Lewis'
life.

His cheeks flush and he turns away. "I don't wanna talk
about it. Not tonight, okay? I need to head back and check
on Petra."

"Hang on a sec," I say and slip behind the bar and
select a bottle of single malt, which I push into his hand.
"For helping."

"I don't want it."

"I have to give you something. To say thanks."

"No need." He grins, then cants his head to the side.
"But … we should toast your Mam."

"She'd be pissed off you dismantled her will, you
know."

He chuckles. "If you agree to a date I think she'd
forgive me."

"Why's that?"

"She went to a lot of effort to arrange one night a year
for me to woo you."

"Wait … this whole setup … all this time …"

"Yeah. She knew I was crazy about you, Selma. I just
— I hadn't the courage to talk to you." He smiles shyly and
takes my hand. "But if you give me a chance, I swear I'll
be as loyal as a dog and —"

I stand on tiptoes and press my lips against his mouth,
quieting him. He returns my kiss with breathtaking
urgency. When we break apart I rest my head against his
warm, solid chest and let the heavy rhythm of his heart
steady me. This man is a whole pint of special with an
angel tears chaser.

"I wanted to kiss you since the day I got stuck on the

roof of the history Portakabin rescuing that lame pigeon and you stole the caretaker's ladder so I could get down," I say.

He laughs and it's the best sound in the world.

You think this is a happy ending, right?

So did I.

And that was my second mistake.

Wrapped in my joy and Lewis' arms, I went back to the cosy barn and left Tommy — brave, quiet, unassuming Tommy Benson, with his tarnished medals, swashbuckling romance novels, and fake lumbago — alone in The Nun's Purse.

His industrial deafness meant he never heard the first molotov cocktail smash through the window and whoomph against the bar. And so Bainbridge — poster boy for rampant Capitalism — finished what Communist torture failed to do so many decades before.

(un)common

Poems

Alix Edwards

In   Love

I wake immune to the drab world outside
drinking your taste your smell your smooth skin
drowning in your smile your soft, laughy voice
feeding you breakfast one strawberry at a time
sinking into your body, spinning
a white-gold sky

lost in infinite forests of emerald trees
Blue Morpho butterflies desert roses
parrots soar above our heads
sapphire macaws sing in ceiba trees
no ceilings or rules can hem us in

Confetti Love

does not
rot
decay
or

spill
like
buckets
of
disappointment

It breathes
with unchoked
lungs
untarred
by gossip

It holds
wedding day
promises

whiteness shot
at the right

angle and the perfect
shutter-speed

Ceyx and Alcyone

Slung ashore, a shipwreck of a man, unclothed by the sea.
Your cracked porcelain skin,
arms wracked wide by the storm.
You leave me,
a grey reminder
of mangled dreams.

My sisters clutch me in a twisted embrace,
comfort is dead.
Your cloaked mother howls into the night.
No-one listens.
Not the sea.
Nor the Gods.
Nothing will save you now.

The Gods have spat you out.
Discordant flutes echo from the bowels of the city.
The gnarled tree stays silent.
I scream into the void.

Punta la Dogana

I needed you yesterday
when our island's shape
became a blur.

I needed you yesterday
when cerulean skies and
rose marble tiles eluded me

I needed you yesterday
on the stone Salute steps
where I could no longer taste
the parma piadine fontina

I needed you yesterday
when I could not mix the peony pink
to paint Piazza San Marco
or its rosy Dolomite clouds

I needed you yesterday
when it hurt to walk alone
down dank alleys
without a Carnevale Mask

       I needed you yesterday
       when loneliness brushed my face
       as I looked for the
       colour we invented here

If

If love had grasped my waist,
my head would float above
the dead weight of my shoulders.

If I could see my name engraved
as *happily married for 50 years,*
I would be someone.

Stuck in this sepia background,
my moments in time
fill negative space.

I am a soulless shape that clings
onto other people's lives,
hoping the focus will shift.

If I lived an unlonely life,
I would not be scrunching
this snail shell underfoot.

Slipstream

Anthony Shapland

A dot travels across the page from word to word.

Patiently, he watches it spiral and meander and turn. A
booklouse. A glue eater, translucent and pale. One of
many, it crawls along *dazzle* to *disguise.*

It reverses –
sight-of-out-stay-to-need-The
– finds the paper's edge and disappears.

He tracks it through the biscuit-brittle long-unopened
book. The insect blends into page after page of details
of animal markings and disguises. Conspicuous patterns
inconspicuous; fooling attackers, confusing rivals.

In a large number of similar objects, an imitator exploits the credibility of its neighbours. There are so many that are obviously authentic that the mind does not take the trouble to suspect pretenders.

—

He spends days like this, standing at the trolley, re-ordering, re-stacking bookshelves.

The library is his haven. High windows of rippled glass filter the glow and fade of unseen cloud-drift. He has no view of the world outside. A darkening around islands of green lampshades and amber pools.

Days settle, motionless. Alone he is in silence, interrupted only by the click-scroll-thrum of microfiche. The dull thump of a weighty book. The crackle and slip of fine paper, swept and turned in dry hands. A cough.

He attends this section often, *Camouflage: Humans and Nature*. Insects that imitate predators to safely pass as dangerous; the bird that borrows noises to elaborate on a mating song, then a section on composers, in turn, notating songs for birds to imitate. Images of dazzle-ships, of combat gear and ghillie suits; of ptarmigan in seasonal plumage, bright hued chameleon, the fish that bob unnoticed among jellyfish and a spider who blinks the courtship pulse of its glow-worm food source.

The lure and the disguise, as quarry evolves with hunter. One thing standing in for another. The imitator slips by, unnoticed and unremarked.

He finds comfort in his everyday routine, his rhythm. Unsure how he fits, he keeps his head down. Reduces the friction he feels in a world that moves too fast.

He slips obstacles to make way for crowds, streams with the least resistance. He unfocuses his eyes, flows along the alien, confident paths. He is an undetected imposter side-stepping the circling, orbiting, waggling bees stuck to the honeyed surface of chattering streets.

With every book returned, he breathes their ease; ease that lingers in aftershave and cigarettes on licked-thumb-turners. He removes bus-ticket markers, unfolds corners where readers quit, finds the stray brackets of dropped eyelashes.

Fiction trickles out, back in, and away again. *New-in* paperbacks, the shallows.

The tide of loans ebbs as books age and move further into the building. Out of the light they sink. Less sought after. Less seen. Into the deep.

He feels like he knows how to be in here. Hurrying is unthinkable, disrespectful. It all takes time. The current slows him to its own measure. He whiles away days in the *stacks*, recovers index-card requests, immersed, breath held. The slow symmetrical glide of cranking wheels open and close the sluice gate of words long-mute in storage.

More obscure titles settle, undisturbed in aisle after aisle.

On Request, far from public inspection. *Specialist* categories.
A locked section marked *Deviant*.

Hidden, he browses alone. He notes the types of male
nakedness kept under key. Photographic nudes that run
and jump, athletic, unashamed. Art books of sculpture.
Sinewy, muscled figures with blank chiselled eyes,
unsighted, anguished. Wistful feminine men look down
in indescribable sorrow. Naked gods scowl from curled
hair and beards, wrestling sea beasts and serpents.

He pictures the mason's hand. Cutting, shaping,
smoothing a hard-as-stone mimic thigh draped with
cloth. Finding the pressure of bone stretching skin, a
curve of flesh in the rock. Pale, accurate stand-ins for
bodies.

The head librarian scrawls borrower's names in a
notebook under *obscene*.

—

Across the library a familiar borrower reads intensely.
An academic, he thinks. The two of them speak through
requests from the Specialist section; a dialogue of
extended loans, months of renewals, years of enquiries.
Each exchange anticipated, hoped for.

He observes, unnoticed. The reader's focus is so complete,
undivided, steady. In dark curly hair, spectacles glint. The
light reflects up onto his familiar downcast face.

What thoughts are in his head?
I wonder how they sound?

His leg bounces slightly. He watches him smile, frown,
pull at his bottom lip and stroke his beard.

*Is he aware of his eyes blinking, his throat swallowing, his lunch moving
through his gut? Does he hear the high pitch of the world in his ears, feel
the weight of his muscles, of his warm body in the chair? Does his thick
beard itch like the one I have grown? Do his bones push and tendons pull
as he reads, fingers resting and feeling the surface of the paper, underlining
the words his eye follows? Does he ever notice me, nearby, being especially
careful, gentle, re-ordering the shelf?*

The silence feels heavy now. Unrippled. Dangerous, dark
water. He wants so much to be seen. He glides the trolley
into the pool of reading lamps.

Then –
Should I be looking this long?
– he veers away.

Aware of his own unseen body, of his empty belly, his
full bladder. Of the bristles rasping at his collar, the
ache in his own neck and the noisy quiet of his inner
voice. *Imposter* – learning to read staring at cereal packets,
ingredients lists, health warnings, adverts. Not clever. Not
even a family bible to prop him up. Here he hides every
day. Performing. Mimicking. Unremarkable.

Maybe I don't feel as other men feel?

– the reader glances up. Smiles.

The trolley wavers. He focuses on the label in front of
him —

Mimicry in Animals. Class: 591.57 Reference – Technical Library.

"Slipstream" is an extract from The Unremark.

Blodeuwedd on the 28

Anastacia Ackers

I've heard it said in rooms that consider themselves important that the Gods and Goddesses of old don't walk these lands anymore. Between mouthfuls of buffet and bullshit, they try and spin the yarn that North Eastern Wales has been lost to the Saes, that borders should be redrawn that leave this area to England.

I inhale and draw upon tales-of-gold-capes-Bryn-yr-Ellyllon-golden-spectres-and-song: I'm here to tell them about Blodeuwedd on the 28.

She carried the look of Havisham and hags and wore it beautifully. Her bee hive may have been more bird's nest, but she kept crumbs in deep pockets to feed the chicks. From Dydd Llun to Dydd Sadwrn, she boarded the 28 at Yr Wyddgrug. It was always the 10:10 (Gwen drives that one) and as she stepped on board, Gwen would grin and print her ticket to Llaneurgain without so much as a word between them, but a whole host more. This dance had been happening for years, way back when the 28 linked Y Fflint to Wrecsam. In those days Blodeuwedd would disembark at Llay and as the bus passed her and the miner's institute, all passengers would wait to watch the wave that Gwen and Blodeuwedd would ride on in farewell. Shirley from Duke Street saw her soulmate Cyril in that wave. Dan from London Road hated soppy shit but caught glimpses of his Gary in that goodbye. Even though the route had changed and links had been lost, Blodeuwedd and Gwen remained the same.

For the thirteen minute journey to Llaneurgain, Gwen would try to keep eyes on the road and Blodeuwedd would try to keep eyes from Gwen, but I'd watch as the camera used for passengers became their way to watch one another. My music would be loud in my ear, but it felt like their gaze was louder, and the stretch of road that passes through Sychdyn became their place, their home, their cynefin. The traffic lights at Llaneurgain felt like a welcome pause for all on board apart from them, for it was the moment before that day's goodbye.

As the bus pulled to a stop at St Eurgain's church, Blodeuwedd would rise slowly, lingering in the moments still on board before stepping into the real world. They'd grin one last time at each other before Blodeuwedd would make her way into the graveyard, and it was at that moment each journey that Gwen would exhale her expectation.

That's how it was for months. Each day, I'd board the 10:10 and watch this play out, and each journey I'd learn a little more. I'd notice the hiding of the ring on

Blodeuwedd's finger, her left hand looking weighed
down. I'd overhear two know-all passengers talking about
Lleu and how he made Blodeuwedd to be his, and wasn't
it a travesty the way she was carrying on. I even caught a
glimpse of Lleu once amidst the bus station chatter and
smells of cattle markets and sglods. He was made from
tradition and the weight of women's crushed dreams, and
as his eyes met mine, there was a moment I'd replay for
all time as the one in which I should have cut him down
where he stood.

It was the day after that Math began boarding, and
herein *all change*.

His steel-toe boots were heavy duty, but hadn't seen
real work in time, and his cocksure habit of greeting
all with a smile-it'll-never-happen greeting meant he
stood out from the get go. Heavy set with hollow eyes, he
looked like he was spoiling (for a fight). Just him setting
foot on this bus made all hairs on the back of my neck
stand on end, and I watched as he tried to make small
talk with Gwen (doesn't buy it), Nancy who sits up front
(turns away) before settling in the seat right opposite
Blodeuwedd. He clocked her straight off, and with a gaze
a hunter gives, he said:

Alright *petal*.

Pretending not to hear, she reached for the crumbs in
her pocket. He cleared his throat and this time it was

Alright *flower*.

These words, meant as terms of endearment in any
other mouth, in his became weapons and we women know
that when wizards want to use their wands it's either fight
or flight. The same time Gwen turned to glare at Math,

Blodeuwedd turned momentarily to meet his eyes and it was in that moment I saw her first feather appear.

Slightly ruffled, Blodeuwedd cast her glance away and even from my back seat view I could see that this was a fork in the road. He began to board daily, always the 10:10, and with each greeting, she'd grow another feather. With each journey, the moments between her and Gwen grew less as Math took up all space. Gwen was powerless from her seat behind the wheel but I, or any of us others on that bus, could have given him what for. Instead I'm left with *what ifs*.

The last time I saw her she had wings, not arms, and her tawny eyes broke as she glanced one last time at Gwen, who hadn't looked her way in time. I watched through the window as she took flight towards the graveyard and heaved as Math became the hero of her tale. Rumour has it Lleu and Math still toast their *victory*.

It was a full year of 10:10s and no her, before I dared to get off the 28 in Llaneurgain. I waited whilst the traffic slowed and as I crossed the threshold into the graveyard, I knew I'd find her here. Footsteps followed feathers, and I spotted her perched in an old yew that held its own tales. She held my gaze before unfurling a wing in the direction of a headstone. Made from Helygain marble, it stood out from all the others and carved into the stone were the words:

Herein lies
BLODEUWEDD
'Made for man,
But belongeth to none'

She'd been tending her own grave for years. She knew better than to lay flowers, and instead had plucked stars from the sky and given them ground. The grass around her grave held universes and constellations, and portents of the world in which we all live and die. In one blade, I watched this story unfold differently.

I exhale, and I'm back in the Room of Important People who are momentarily questioning their own sanity, before questioning mine and conversation returns to the age-old discussion of which fucking cae they're building on next.

Little do they know.

Their bones are my stars and Blodeuwedd's grave needs tending.

The Green Coat

Rosy Adams

The first time Mia saw a dragon, she was at work. It was near closing time and the day was already fading to dusk. She had taken the bags of rubbish out the back, pushing the bar on the door with her hip because her hands were full. Down the steps, into the narrow street of back doors where the large wheelie bins huddled in groups of two or three. She lifted the lid of the one closest and slung the bags in one by one.

It was when she turned to go back inside that she saw it, nestled in a pool of shadow in the lee of the steps. It was much smaller than she had thought a dragon would be; about the size of a large dog. The parts of it that were illuminated by the street lights were white overlaid with a shimmer of silver. The eyes were cloudy globes of moonstone with no discernible pupil, yet she could tell that the dragon was looking at her. Half afraid, half enchanted, she stood and stared into its eyes for what seemed like hours, but when the dragon blinked and turned away it was still early evening and nothing had changed.

With a flick of its tail the dragon disappeared into the dark corner where the steps met the brick wall. When she stepped closer to see where it had gone the corner wasn't so dark after all and there was nothing to see but a collection of rubbish gathered by the wind.

She put it out of her mind and returned to the kitchen, which had to be cleaned ready for the morning before she could go home.

She was the last out, as always. By the time she had set the alarm and locked up it was full dark and there was a mean gusty wind that found all the gaps in her coat. She crossed her arms tight and hunched her neck into the collar like a tortoise, wishing she'd thought to bring a scarf.

The shop windows on the High Street were already filled with Christmas decorations and lights. She walked slowly, looking at each display and deciding what she would buy if she had money to spare. In the window of the most expensive clothes shop in town (the shop she had never set foot in, even just to look) was a tailored wool coat with glossy black buttons, nipped in at the waist and flared over the hips. It was the vivid green of moss on a riverbank. Every evening after work she paused by that window to look at it, imagining what sort of person she would be with a coat like that, and every evening she would walk on, reminding herself that it was utterly impractical and she didn't want it anyway.

She walked down the high street to the bus stop. This part of the town centre was shabby and populated mainly with bookies and discount shops. Next to the bus shelter stood an unusually tall person with skin that made her think of river-smoothed stone, and a cloud of tangled pale hair. Unsettling eyes of lichen yellow-grey met hers and she felt a jolt like an electric shock. It was hard to say if it was anxiety or excitement. The stone person dipped their head in what seemed to her as an acknowledgement, then they took a step back and faded away until there was only mist, which the wind whipped away in moments.

She thought perhaps she should be worried about seeing things that didn't exist, but she was too tired to care. She was tired all the time. The days of her life passed in a grey fog of work. Work at the café and work at home. Cleaning, cooking and taking care of others. She would have liked to go to bed and sleep for a hundred years.

The bus arrived and she took a seat with a sigh of relief. It jerked and swayed its way through the suburbs, eventually depositing her a short walk from her house. The streets were empty, but the wind made a show of noise and movement in the trees and the drifts of fallen leaves. The moon was near full and it lit up the racing clouds in purple and navy blue.

She kept thinking that she could see things out of the corners of her eyes but when she looked straight at them they became nothing more than windblown leaves and litter. She was relieved when she reached the house.

The front garden was a mess. The lawn had been left too long in the summer and now it was humped with weeds, and the path had almost disappeared under a blanket of couch grass and bramble. Pound-shop solar garden lights stood askew amongst the undergrowth. The ones that still worked had a pale and sickly glow that was worse than nothing at all.

It occurred to Mia that her husband had spent more time maintaining the garden when he was working full-time than now, when he wasn't working at all.

The damp that came with autumn had made the wood of the door swell and warp so that she had to shove with her shoulder to open it, then again to force it closed once she was inside.

The hallway was dark, and the only sound she could hear was the television in the living room. The kitchen was also dark, and there was no sign that anyone had made dinner.

She hung her coat up in the hall and went straight to the fridge to find something to cook, knowing that if she sat down for even a moment she wouldn't be able to get up and going again. A bitter swell of resentment was overwhelmed by the wave of guilt that came immediately after. It wasn't his fault, she told herself. Everyone was getting laid off these days, and it was no wonder he was feeling low. Not that she didn't feel low herself, but there were things that had to be done, and there was no-one else to do them.

By the time everyone had eaten and she had finished the washing up it was 10pm. She leaned her elbows on the edge of the sink and looked at her reflection in the night-black window. The dark glass gave her face a touch of glamour. Her eyes appeared deep and mysterious and all the fine lines of weariness around them were smoothed away. To either side of her reflection she saw what appeared to be large golden lamps, growing slowly brighter until they were all she could see.

When Mia woke up she found that she was lying on the kitchen floor, cheek pressed to the cold tiles. She lay there for awhile because she couldn't think of a good enough reason to get up. From this angle she could see underneath the cupboard where old cobwebs and shrivelled scraps of food had drifted. It was a long time since she had last done a deep clean and quite honestly she was starting to question the point of it all. It would only get dirty again.

Eventually her discomfort outweighed her exhaustion and so she pulled herself up to her feet. The window was dark. No-one seemed to have noticed her moment of unconsciousness. Her husband had returned to the television and her two children to their rooms, hopefully to bed, ready for college in the morning but most likely they were still up, in thrall to their smart phones.

She imagined it as a house in stasis. Whenever she left or returned her husband would be watching television in his dressing gown, a lukewarm cup of tea by his chair, and her teenaged children would be closeted in their rooms with the devices that were their portals to other worlds. She wondered how long it would take them to notice if anything happened to her, and it made her sad to think that it would probably be when they ran out of food and clean clothes.

It was still dark when Mia left for work the next day.
At the bus stop, she and her fellow commuters stood
in companionable early morning gloom. She enjoyed
the bus journeys, even though the seats were scratchy
and there was a persistent smell of stale cigarette smoke
despite no-one having lit up inside since the smoking
ban, and sometimes there were strange passengers with no
concept of boundaries. Despite that, it was a time when
she could relax.

Outside the hazed windows the town began to take
shape in the pre-dawn light. There were indistinct
flickers of movement and flashes of colour and she wiped
away the condensation to see a motley parade of people
(creatures?) all shapes and sizes, playing on strange
instruments, spinning and jumping and dancing.

She looked around to see if anyone else had noticed
them but no-one was looking out of the window. When
she looked back the bus had passed them by, if they were
even there in the first place. Her heart beat faster and she
felt hot and restless. Perhaps she was having a hot flash. It
was an unwelcome reminder of her age that such a thing
was even a possibility.

By the time she got to work the parade of people
seemed like something seen in a dream, and in fact, she
suspected that she had drifted off for a bit. Still, it played
on her mind, so much so that she messed up several
breakfast orders. The manager was so disturbed by her
uncharacteristic behaviour that he told her to take the
afternoon off.

The sensible thing to do would have been to go home
and catch up on all the things that needed doing around

the house, but instead she found herself walking in the opposite direction. She wasn't going anywhere in particular, just walking for the sake of it.

She walked through the older part of town, the part that was once a village. She walked past thick-walled cottages with low roofs and small windows. An old graveyard curtained with yew trees. A wide green space with a rush-fringed pond where people walked dogs and played football. She had taken the children there when they were young.

She walked past the larger, newer houses, with larger, newer cars outside. She looked at the houses as she passed them and tried to imagine living in one of them but she couldn't. All that space. And they probably had cleaners come in once a week. It made her terribly sad to think that she had no idea what she would do if she had the sort of life that she imagined the residents to have.

She noticed a woman in the window of the nearest house. The woman was staring at her, and she realised that she had been standing still and gazing at the house for some minutes. Mia hurried away, tucking her head down, heat rushing to her cheeks.

She was heading back to the centre of town to catch the bus home when she saw the dragon. It was a different one. Bigger. It was curled around the gable end of a derelict cottage. Its legs were stretched out and its head rested on the ground between them. It reminded her of a greyhound, all long-boned and lean-muscled, if a greyhound had grown as big as a stretch limousine.

She wondered if she might be going mad. If so, it wasn't nearly as unpleasant a process as she thought it should be. The dragon was beautiful. It was flame-red, fading to apricot on its belly, with membranous wings neatly folded along its back.

Perhaps it sensed her watching because it raised its head and opened its eyes to look back at her. *I should be afraid,* she thought, but she was enchanted. The dragon's eyes were molten gold. It blinked slowly. She wondered what would happen if she were to approach it. She was more afraid that it would not be real than she was of being hurt. At least if it left a mark it would be proof that she wasn't going crazy.

Before she could move closer the dragon turned and flowed away behind the cottage. She ran after it but there was nothing there but a drift of autumn leaves. She felt bereft, as if something important had died.

She stood there, tears brimming and blurring her vision, until her fingers and toes were numb with cold. Then she walked to the doctor's surgery and made an appointment, before catching the bus home.

Mia wakes. It's dark. She is in a bed and someone is asleep next to her. She can hear his loud steady breathing, almost a snore. She can't remember how she got here or who is lying beside her. She counts down from ten and by the time she gets to one it has come back to her. She is at home and the man in her bed is her husband.

She knows there's no point in trying to go back to sleep; insomnia seems to be one of the side-effects of her medication. She hasn't seen anything unusual since the dragon with the golden eyes, but sometimes she feels confused, especially when she first wakes up.

She eases herself out of bed and goes downstairs. The glowing figures on the cooker tell her that it's just after four. Her husband will get up at six to go to work. When the doctor diagnosed her with psychotic depression, the shock of it roused him from his melancholy and he went out and found himself a new job with a landscaping firm.

The kitchen is spotless. No clutter or dirty washing up, and all the surfaces have been wiped down. Her children have started helping around the house, and although the bulk of the housework still falls to her, she appreciates their efforts. They will be up around seven, getting ready to catch the bus to college at quarter past eight.

She knows that things are better than they have been for a long time, but most of the time she feels flat, as if she is watching her life playing on a television screen. The doctor tells her not to worry, it's just a side-effect of the drugs, and it's very important that she continues to take them, even if she thinks she doesn't need them. Especially if she thinks she doesn't need them.

Today is her day off. This is part of the plan to make her normal again. One day off a week to engage in a meaningful occupation. Her occupational therapy assessment was held at a mental health centre with a kind woman who looked barely older than her own children. She asked Mia what sort of things she most liked doing. Mia couldn't answer her. There wasn't a single thing she could think of that she did purely for own enjoyment, except perhaps looking at the green coat in the shop window, but that seemed so pathetic and trivial that she couldn't admit to it.

After an hour of discussion the best suggestion the

therapist could make was that Mia take art classes, as it had been a subject she liked in school, so now she goes to the local college once a week and spends two hours in an art studio with a mismatched group of other adults and an sweet earnest tutor who is young enough to still be enthusiastic.

She takes her sketchbook from her bag in the hall and goes to the living room. She sits in the pool of light from a single table lamp and works on her newest drawing; her memory of the dragon with the golden eyes. She doesn't show this sketchbook to anyone. She has been encouraged to "move on" and "put the past behind her" and she knows that sketching her hallucinations is not something that she should be doing, but the memory haunts her and she thinks that maybe this will help lay it to rest.

In class, she paints anodyne watercolours of scenes around the town that people can look at and say "oh, that's the pond on the green, how clever you are!"

It's a pleasant enough pastime, and she has discovered that she can sketch scenes quickly and well. Before Christmas she painted a number of miniature landscapes with a winter theme which made perfect presents for friends and family. Everyone else loved them, but to her they looked bland and lifeless.

The dragon in her picture seems to look at her, just like the one in her memory.

When the house begins to stir she puts her sketchbook away.

After everyone else has left the house she steps out into an unseasonably mild morning. There are no strange figures or mythical creatures to be seen on her walk to the bus stop. Everything is relentlessly normal. A young mother struggles with a toddler who seems intent on escaping his reins. It ends with both of them flushed and cross, the mother tapping at her phone and the child lying on the pavement, wailing at the injustice of his defeat.

She feels sympathy for him. He's at the age where he still sees magic and adventure everywhere around him, but he's not allowed to seek it out.

She takes the bus to the college entrance. There is a stone archway, a remnant of an older collection of buildings. As she is about to walk underneath she sees something move in the corner of her eye. She looks up and sees the ink-black dragon draped over the arch. It stares at her, and its eyes are smoky blue orbs. Other students pass her, oblivious to the sinuous creature hanging above their heads.

She knows she should be upset that the drugs are no longer working, but instead she feels a surging delight and she's sure this can't be bad. How can it be depression when she feels so happy?

The dragon's tail dangles low enough for her to reach. This time she doesn't hesitate. She grasps the end before it can disappear. It's solid. Warm and muscular like the body of a snake. The dragon flicks it away, much like a cat would. It rises to its feet, gripping the ornamented stone with curved claws, opening wings of bone and sinew, and skin stretched tight, the black shading through indigo to lilac where the light shines through it. It leaps into the air and sideslips on a breath of wind, appearing impossibly light. A piece of stone decoration breaks off from the force of its take off and falls close to her feet.

The dragon circles higher and higher until she can no longer see it. She picks up the piece of stone. It's a carved leaf, part of a winding vine design. She puts it in her bag and goes to her art class where she ignores the model posing in the centre of the room and sketches her memory of the dragon on the arch while it's still fresh in her mind. She brushes off the tentative questions of the tutor, and when the class has finished she rolls up her picture and tucks it under her arm, walking out without a word to anyone.

She feels more purposeful than she can ever remember being in her life, although she has no idea what that purpose is. Only that it is becoming more urgent as time passes.

At home she goes through her usual routine but her mind is somewhere else. At bedtime, she stands in front of the bathroom mirror, a glass of water in one hand and her daily dose of medication in the other. What good is it, really? It isn't doing what it's supposed to do, and does she even want that anyway?

She tips the pills back into the bottle and returns it to its place in the cupboard. It's close to midnight but she is wide awake so she goes downstairs and puts her worn old coat over her pyjamas. She steps out into a cold moonless night. The sky is clear and the stars shine brilliant as splinters of glass. Frost has already formed on the row of parked cars. She trails her fingers over them as she walks, enjoying the ice-burn on her skin.

At the end of the street is a collection of tall bony creatures, rough-haired and pale. At first glance they look like horses but she's not surprised when she notices the spiralling horns that sprout from the broad foreheads. As she draws closer they startle, dark eyes edged with white crescents and flaring nostrils blowing plumes of steam. They wheel away, cloven hooves thudding on the tarmac and tangled tails flying like pennants.

She wonders if the myth about virgins is true and if that's why they ran from her. She walks on, and the town at night appears to her as a forest, the shadow and starlight rendering the ordinary as new and strange.

She sees otherworldly people, winged, furred, and scaled, with claws, hooves, tails, horns. Eyes slit-pupiled as a cat's, or birdlike round and yellow. Even blood-red, like nothing she's ever seen before. They watch her walk.

Despite the cold she slips out of her coat, hanging it on the wing mirror of a builder's van. She steps out of her slippers, leaving them on someone's doorstep, placed neatly side by side. She savours the shock of the icy pavement against the soles of her feet. Her pyjamas go next, draped over a hedge. In the morning people will puzzle over them, and eventually the police will take them away in evidence bags to be interrogated.

She wears her skin loosely. It wrinkles at the elbows and knees, before peeling away in ribbons to expose the vivid green beneath. She feels an unfolding, within and without, extra nerves and muscles twitching and flexing. She stretches out her wings and they are like new leaves in springtime. The pins-and-needles sensation of blood flowing to new areas of her body is a painful pleasure, and when it subsides she can feel every tiny current of air as it whispers against her skin.

No more than a push from her legs and she is in the air, balancing on a breath, and above her they are waiting. Silver-white, red, and black.

A Manifesto for Making Work amidst Sheer Fuckwittery

Anastacia Ackers

- Drink hope as though it is coffee. Sip galvanisation like it's a brew.
- Remember the reasons why you do what you do, tattoo those across your heart and clutch them tightly amidst the onslaught of fuckwittery.
- Pull the words and worlds from the ether – maybe you're the only one who can.
- Use headlines as kindle and turn those fuckers into a fire that will burn their house down.
- For every door that's slammed in your face, kick another in with your unapologetic self.
- In this climate of perpetual emergency, art is the antidote.
- Sit your inner critic down and tell it NOW IS NOT THE TIME.
- Co-create with your community and remember art is the town hall, the village green and everything in between.
- In the rough times, find your tonic.
- Start, right now.

Author biographies

Anastacia Ackers is a writer, theatre maker and facilitator from North East Wales. She was the co-creator of National Theatre Wales TEAM Wrecsam production, *A Proper Ordinary Miracle*. She also works alongside Outside Lives, a not-for-profit social enterprise based in Maeshafn, Flintshire and is currently supporting the LikeMinded group for people living with dementia, as part of the Dementia Engagement and Empowerment Project (DEEP). Anastacia is passionate about history and mythology and co-creating alongside communities. She is working on her first piece of creative non-fiction exploring the Taith Pererin Gogledd Cymru/North Wales Pilgrim's Way.

Rosy Adams grew up in Y Bannau Brycheiniog where she spent most of her time in the library or up the mountain. She has a passion for myth and fairy tale, the influence of which shows in her own writing. Her stories have been published by *Writing Magazine, Muswell Press, Grim & Gilded, Trash to Treasure Literary, Maenad Literary Journal,* and *Lucent Dreaming*. She is working on a short story collection and two (or maybe three) novels.

Kittie Belltree's debut poetry collection *Sliced Tongue and Pearl Cufflinks* is published by Parthian (2019). Her poems, short fiction and reviews have appeared in numerous journals and anthologies including *The Morning Star, Planet, The Brown Envelope Book* (Caparisan, 2020), *Cast a Long Shadow* (Honno, 2022), *Heartland* (Parthian, 2019) and *Cut on the Bias* (Honno, 2010). She has just completed her first novel. When not writing, Kittie works as a Specialist Tutor for neurodivergent students and delivers collaborative creative learning and wellbeing projects in the community with organisations including Literature Wales, Arts Council Wales and Disability Arts Cymru.

Jon Doyle is a writer based in Port Talbot, South Wales. His work has appeared in *Short Fiction, Hobart, Ploughshares Online, The Rumpus,* and *3:AM Magazine* among other places, and he runs the music publication *Various Small Flames*. Find him on Twitter @Jon_Doyle or on his website: jon-doyle.co.uk.

Alix Edwards uses photography, large-scale paintings and spoken word to explore untold histories, resilience, loss and shame. Her art has been exhibited in England, Wales, Spain and LA and her poetry has been published in *Penny Thoughts, haus-a-rest, Poetry Wales* and *Cardiff Review*. In 2018 she founded Company of Words spoken word events to encourage those new to writing to perform their work. Her mission is to empower people through creativity, and she has run arts projects for the Salvation Army, Women's Aid. FiLiA and Treorchy Time Capsule. Alix has recently completed a poetry pamphlet which challenges assumptions about domestic abuse and is currently writing a YA novel set in Victorian Cardiff. She loves walking barefoot on the sand, swimming in the sea and dancing to salsa music.

Simone Greenwood grew up in rural Cumbria and has lived the last two decades in South East Wales. She had a "best of times, worst of times" childhood (see Kayleigh Llewellyn's In My Skin for a flavour) and spent a year in the nineties living in a cult (yes, she's writing a screenplay about THAT). Once a primary school teacher, Simone now freelances in publishing and arts administration, alongside writing. She's working on several children's novels, as well as screenplays. Neuro-divergency is her superpower … and what she blames for her house being a mess.

Ben Huxley is a writer based in North East Wales. He spans the arts, from acting to video game journalism, but fiction is the craft he adores most. His writing is inspired by his upbringing in Colwyn Bay, the mountains and ridges of Snowdonia, and the (mostly Japanese) games he grew up with. Ben is currently working on his second novel and looking for a home for his first.

Bridget Keehan grew up in Bournemouth but now lives in Cardiff, where she works as a theatre producer and director. She is the founding director of Papertrail Theatre Company. She has written short stories and articles and has been published by *The Guardian, Planet* and *Wales Arts Review. Identity Theft* is her first novel. It's about 15-year-old Aisling, who yearns to be an actress but ends up a fraudster.

Ciaran Keys was born in North Wales in 1986. His family moved around the north of England until his Dad died and his Mum took them to Ireland. His inheritance from his Dad was a lifelong obsession with science fiction. He decided he was a writer while roaming around County Clare. On returning to Wales he was momentarily distracted for twenty years before screwing his head back on and trying again. He now lives in Liverpool with his wife and their Pomeranian, who conveniently share one personality, and he tries to write without making a big ordeal of it.

Amy Kitcher lives in the South Wales Valleys and divides her time unevenly between her two jobs, her two children and her two passions: reading and writing. She can talk about books in four different languages and has a Masters degree in modern warfare. Amy has been writing for almost a decade and was named as one of Literature Wales' Representing Wales 2022/23 cohort. Her poetry and short stories have been published in various online magazines and anthologies.
T: @amykitcher I: @amykitcher

Frankie Parris is a trans writer, musician and filmmaker living in London (via Cardiff). Their work is often a reflection on personal experience, grappling with themes of identity, mental illness, love and relationships. They take inspiration from writers such as The New York Poets, Kim Hiorthøy and Miranda July. Frankie's work has been featured in *Spacecraft Mag, Powders Press* and in exhibitions at Dyddiau Du, Cardiff Umbrella and The Hearth Gallery. They have spent the last year mentored by Peter Scalpello as part of Literature Wales' Representing Wales programme for underrepresented writers. They have recently finished shooting their first short film as well as a collection of poetry, *Chaos November* which they hope to release later this year.

Anthony Shapland grew up in the Rhymney Valley. He is co-founder of g39, Cardiff, where he works. He was part of the Representing Wales 2022/23 Cohort with mentoring support from Cynan Jones. He was shortlisted for the Rhys Davies award for "Foolscap", part of the anthology *Cree*, published by Parthian. A non-fiction essay, "Meantime", appears in the anthology *Cymru & I* published by Seren. He was selected for the Hay Writers at Work programme in 2023 and his debut novel *A Room Above a Shop* will be published by Granta in Spring 2024.